COLLINS·LONGMAN

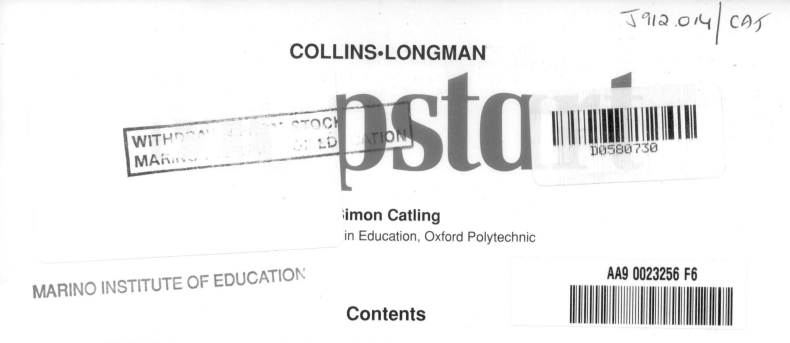

Upstart

Simon Catling

in Education, Oxford Polytechnic

Contents

Mapping the locality

Ⓐ

Block of flats, numbers 1-31

Terraced house, number 22

Detached house, number 1A

A is an **oblique aerial photo**. In the centre you can see a block of flats. The area around the flats is called Hillmead. It is in the north of the town of Norwich. Hillmead is a residential area. The roads are lined by people's homes. Photos **B**, **C** and **D** show three types of home in Hillmead.

E is a **vertical aerial photo** of the same area. **H** is a map of Hillmead. Use the key to see what the symbols on the map mean.

On the map and aerial photos find where the homes in photos **B**, **C** and **D** are in Hillmead.

1 What are the numbers of the homes on each side of the home in photo **C**?
2 Does photo **B** show the back or the front of the flats you can see in the centre of **A**?
3 Find the home in **D** on map **H**. Draw its shape.
4 How many rows of terraced houses are there
5 The building in photo **F** is not in Hillmead. Find it on map **H**. Which roads go past it?
6 Look at photo **G**. Use **A**, **E** and **H** to work out where it is. What is the number of the home front of which the photo was taken?
7 Imagine you are walking from flat 1 to house number 114. Describe which way you would go and what you would pass on the way.

E

F

G

KEY

▨	Homes
▨	Garages and sheds
▨	Pub
▨	Church
▨	Gardens
▨	Grass
▨	Car park and driveway
‒ ‒ ‒	Road and pavement
- - -	Path
⊥⊤⊥	Fences
● ●	Trees

Park House

Oak Grove Church

HILLMEAD

CATTON GROVE ROAD

OAK LANE

Grid references

Norwich

KEY

	Homes
	Garages and sheds
	Shops
	Pub
	Church
	Gardens
	Allotment gardens
	Grass
	Car park and driveway
-----	Road and pavement
-------	Path
	Roundabout
	Fences
	Trees

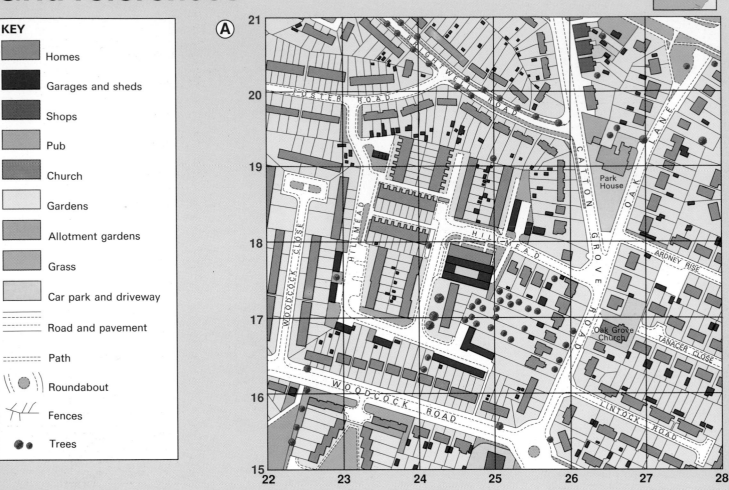

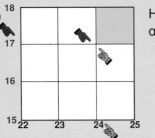

Map **A** shows more of the area around Hillmead. **Grid lines** have been drawn over the map. Each line is numbered. Along the **bottom** of the map the **black** numbers increase from left to right. They name the vertical lines. Up the **side** of the map the **red** numbers increase from the bottom to the top. They name the horizontal lines. These numbers help to name the **grid squares** on the map.

To find grid square **24,17** on map **A** you need to follow these instructions. **B** shows you how.
* Put a finger on number **24** at the bottom of map **A**.
* Put another finger on number **17** at the side of map **A**.
* Move both fingers along the grid lines. Where the two lines cross is the lower left corner of grid square **24,17**.

This is the **four-figure grid reference** for the grid square containing the block of flats in Hillmead.

How to find a grid square.

Now find Oak Grove Church. To tell someone its **four-figure grid reference** you must:
* Put your fingers on the grid lines at the lower left corner of the grid square the church is in.
* Follow the vertical and horizontal lines to the edge of the map with each finger.
* Read number **26** at the bottom of the vertical line first, then number **16** at the side of the horizontal line.

1 Name three features in grid square **22,16**.
2 Give the grid reference for the roundabout.
3 Choose two grid squares. Give their grid references and name three features in each.

Compass directions

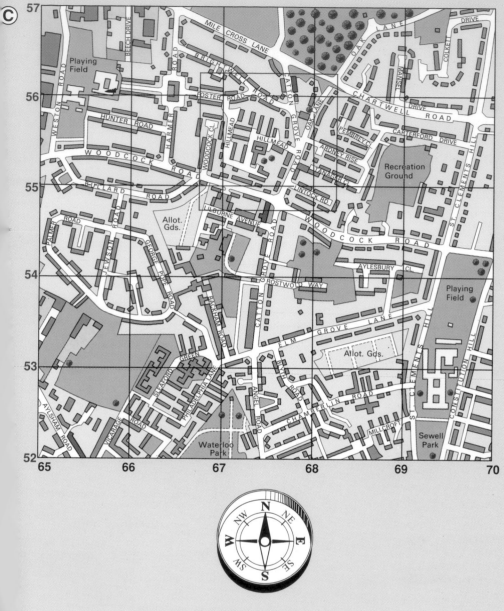

KEY

	Buildings
	Shops
	School
	Church
	Factory
	Gardens
	Park and grass
	Open ground
	Road
	Path
	Trees
Allot. Gds.	Allotment gardens
CL.	Close
RD.	Road

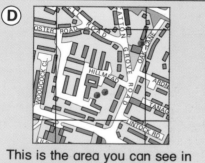

This is the area you can see in map **A**. Find it in map **C**.

Map **C** shows much more of the area around Hillmead. Use the key to see what the symbols on the map mean.

Hillmead is at grid reference **67,55**. It is in the north of the area shown on the map. North is a **compass direction**. Compass directions help us to say in which **direction** places are. You can use the compass below map **C** to work out the directions.

...nd Hillmead. To the north of Hillmead you can ...e Foster Road and Brightwell Road. There is a ...creation ground to the east of Hillmead. Find ...e allotment gardens southwest of Hillmead.

1. Which road goes along the east side of Hillmead?
2. Go south along Catton Grove Road to Rostwold Way **67,53**. Is Rostwold Way east or west of Catton Grove Road?
3. Find Jewson Road in grid square **65,54**. Is it southeast or southwest of Hillmead?
4. In which direction is Hillmead from the school in grid square **69,52**?
5. What are the buildings on the southwest of the junction of Woodcock Road and Catton Grove Road in grid square **67,54** used for?

5

Measuring on the map

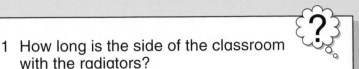

A is a plan of a classroom. Use the key to see what the symbols show is in the classroom.

The classroom plan has been drawn to **scale**. You can work out the size of the actual classroom by using the **scale bar** below map **A**. The scale bar is like a ruler. It is used to **measure** distances on the plan. On this scale bar 1 centimetre on the plan measures half a metre (50 centimetres) in the real classroom.

In plan **A** you can use the scale bar to measure the length and width of the classroom and of different pieces of furniture. You can also use it to measure how near or far apart features in the room are.

1 How long is the side of the classroom with the radiators?
2 How long and wide is the Reading Area?
3 What is the length of the plant tray?
4 Name three objects in the classroom less than 1 metre long.
5 How far is it in a straight line from the classroom door to the plant tray?
6 How far is it from the chair in the Reading Area to the sink?
7 What is the longest piece of furniture in **A**?

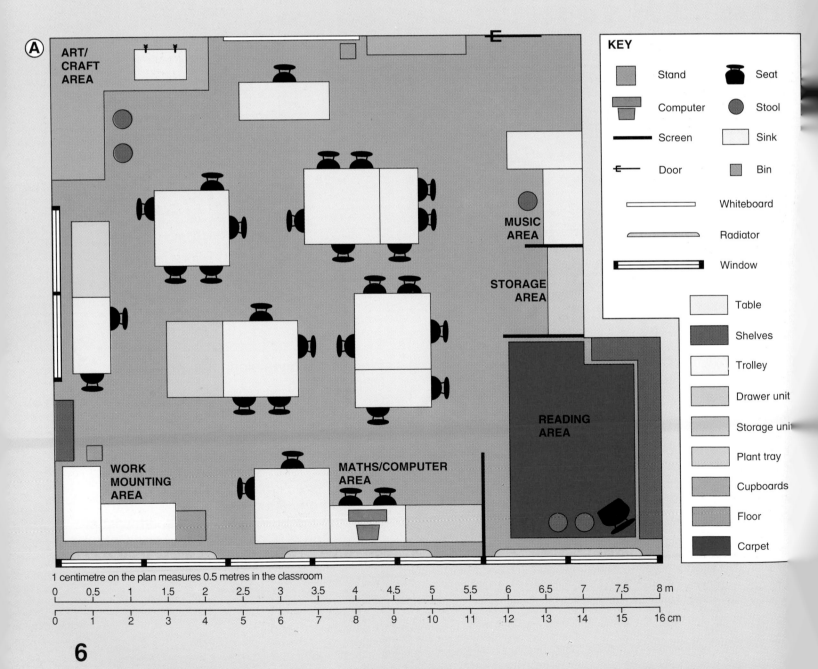

B

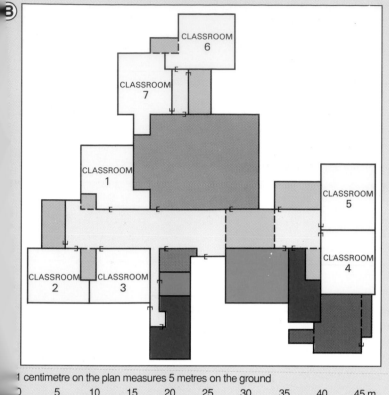

CLASSROOM 6

CLASSROOM 7

CLASSROOM 1

CLASSROOM 5

CLASSROOM 2

CLASSROOM 3

CLASSROOM 4

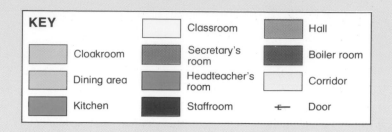

B and **C** are plans of St. Albans' School in Harlow. Plan **B** shows the main school building. Its scale bar shows that 1 cm on the plan measures 5m of the real school building. Plan **C** is drawn to a smaller scale to show all the school grounds. The scale bar under **C** shows that 1 cm on the plan measures 10 m of the real school grounds.

1 How long is the corridor in **B**?
2 How far is it from the door of classroom 2 to the door of classroom 5 in **B**?
3 In **C** how long is the playground?
4 How long is the path on the west side of the school grounds?

1 centimetre on the plan measures 5 metres on the ground

0	5	10	15	20	25	30	35	40	45 m
0	1	2	3	4	5	6	7	8	9 cm

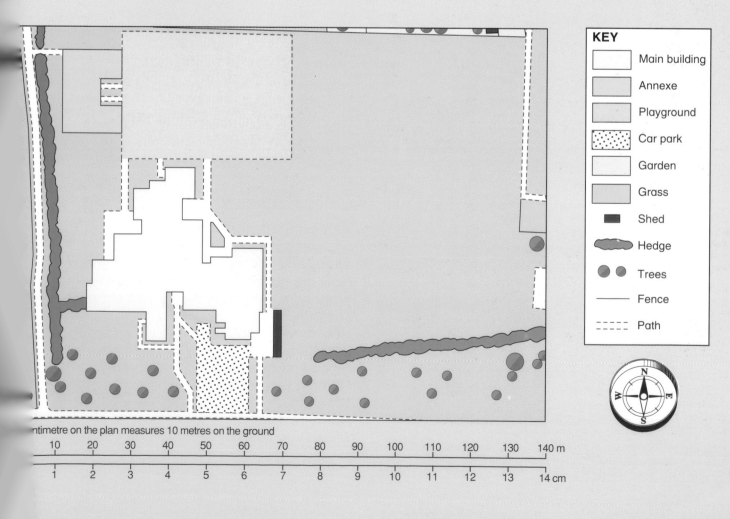

KEY

- Main building
- Annexe
- Playground
- Car park
- Garden
- Grass
- Shed
- Hedge
- Trees
- Fence
- Path

1 centimetre on the plan measures 10 metres on the ground

10	20	30	40	50	60	70	80	90	100	110	120	130	140 m
1	2	3	4	5	6	7	8	9	10	11	12	13	14 cm

Using maps in a local survey

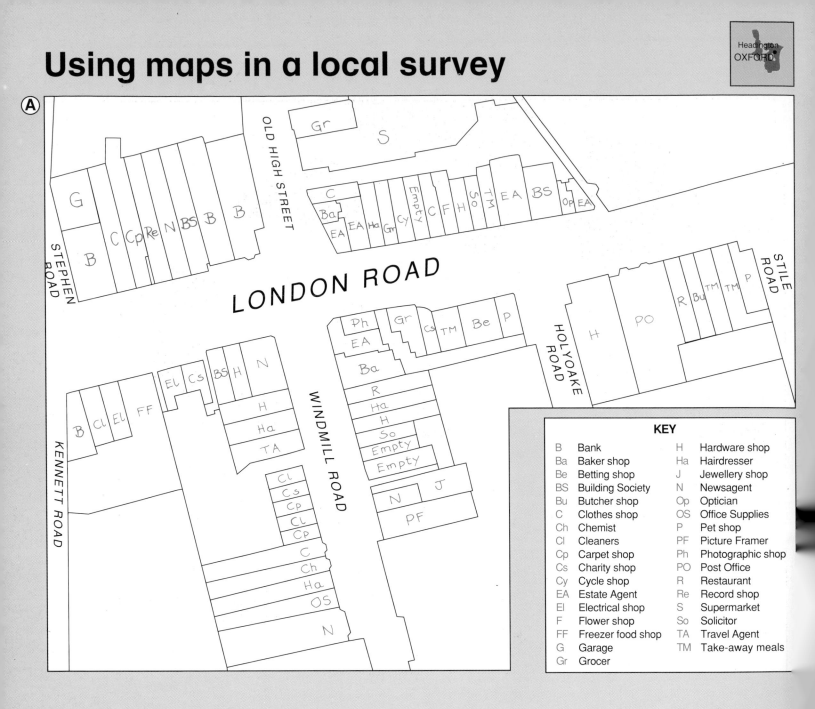

KEY

B	Bank	H	Hardware shop
Ba	Baker shop	Ha	Hairdresser
Be	Betting shop	J	Jewellery shop
BS	Building Society	N	Newsagent
Bu	Butcher shop	Op	Optician
C	Clothes shop	OS	Office Supplies
Ch	Chemist	P	Pet shop
Cl	Cleaners	PF	Picture Framer
Cp	Carpet shop	Ph	Photographic shop
Cs	Charity shop	PO	Post Office
Cy	Cycle shop	R	Restaurant
EA	Estate Agent	Re	Record shop
El	Electrical shop	S	Supermarket
F	Flower shop	So	Solicitor
FF	Freezer food shop	TA	Travel Agent
G	Garage	TM	Take-away meals
Gr	Grocer		

You can use a map to make a **survey**.
Map **A** shows what was found out about some of the buildings on London Road, Old High Street and Windmill Road in Headington, Oxford.

A blank **base map** which showed the outline of the buildings was used for the survey.
On the base map information was written about the **service** in each building.
A letter code was used to **record** the information easily. The key shows what the letters mean. The information on the map tells us about the services in each of the buildings, not their names.

Map **A** is an **annotated** map. It shows that most of the buildings are used as shops.

1 Name six different types of shops you can see in **A**.
2 Along which street are there most shops?
3 How are baker shops shown in **A**?
4 What type of shop is the largest shop you can see in **A**?
5 How many shops are there which sell food?
6 Is there a shop where you could have a bicycle repaired?
7 Name a type of shop which people might visit every day.
8 Name two buildings which are not shops, where you can buy things.

Map **B** has been coloured using the information from annotated map **A**. This has been done by grouping similar types of **services** together.

On map **A** you can see that there are several shops which sell household goods, like carpets, electrical goods and hardware. This is one type of service. These shops have been grouped, or **classified**, together because they have the same **function**. On map **B** they have all been coloured dark green. The colour symbols in the key show you how the services have been classified. Another group, or **category**, is specialist services, which includes banks, building societies and estate agents.

1 What type of shop is shown by purple on map **B**?
2 How are hairdressers shown on map **B**?
3 How many hairdressers are there in the area shown on map **A**?
4 What type of shop can you see most of on map **B**?
5 Use map **A** to help you name the types of food and drink shops that have been classified together on map **B**?
6 On map **B** are there more shops selling household goods than food and drink?
7 Name all the services shown on map **A** which have been classified as specialist services on map **B**.

Using maps as records and plans

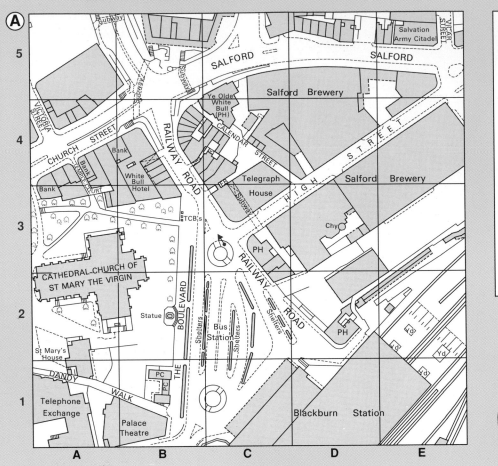

KEY

▭	Buildings
----	Road and pavement
═══	Railway
▯	Steps
⌂	Trees
Chy	Chimney
FB	Foot bridge
PC	Public convenience
PH	Public house
TCB	Telephone call box
Yd	Yard

1 centimetre on the map measures
25 metres on the ground

```
0      25      50      75    100 m
|-------|-------|-------|-------|
0       1       2       3     4 cm
```

Map **A** shows the area around Railway Road in the town of Blackburn. Photo **B** shows what Railway Road looks like. The arrow in grid square **C3** shows where photo **B** was taken from, looking northwest. Map **A** and photo **B** show how Railway Road looks now.

Photo **C** shows how Railway Road looked in 1907. See how many changes to the street you can spot.

Map **D** is even older. It shows Railway Road in 1893. By **comparing** maps **A** and **D** you can see what changes have taken place in the area around Railway Road. This is because the maps are records of how the area looks at the time that the maps are made.

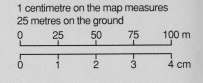

1 Name three features that appear on maps **A** and **D**, even though they have changed a little.
2 In which direction are you looking along Railway Road in photo **C**?
3 Use the scale bar to measure how long Railway Road is in map **A**. Is High Street longer or shorter?

10

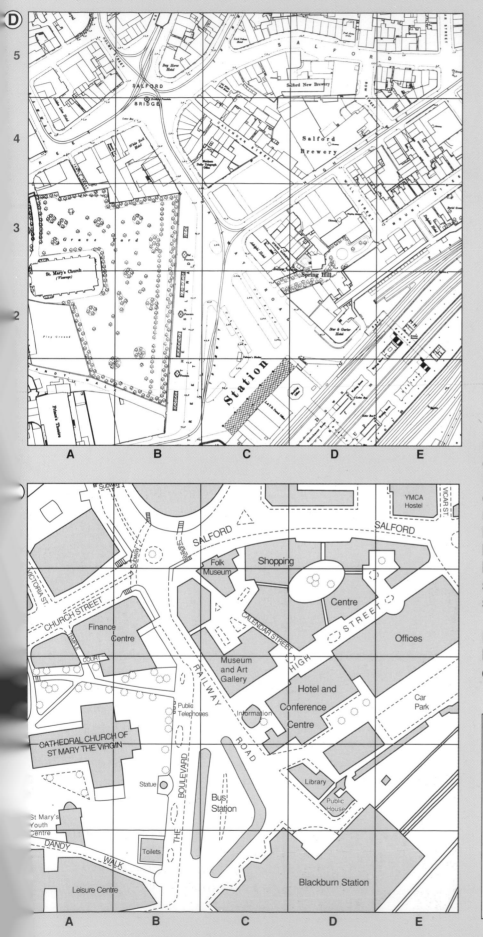

Ⓓ

KEY

Glass covered area

Road and pavement

Railway

Tramway

Trees

Lamppost

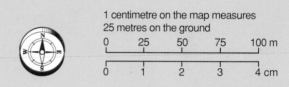

1 centimetre on the map measures
25 metres on the ground

0	25	50	75	100 m

0	1	2	3	4 cm

Map **E** is another map of the same area you can see in maps **A** and **D**. But it has been drawn to show how the area might look in the future. It is an imaginary map that shows a plan of how the area might look if some of the buildings were pulled down and new buildings put up. Look at it carefully to see what features remain that you can see on map **A**.

Planners draw maps like **E** to show how changes might affect what people can do and the way a place looks.

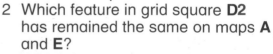

1 Find the Folk Museum on map **E**. What does map **A** show it is at present?
2 Which feature in grid square **D2** has remained the same on maps **A** and **E**?
3 Which feature on map **D** remains on map **E**?
4 Compare maps **A** and **E** to name three more changes which are shown in map **E**.

Using maps to plan a journey

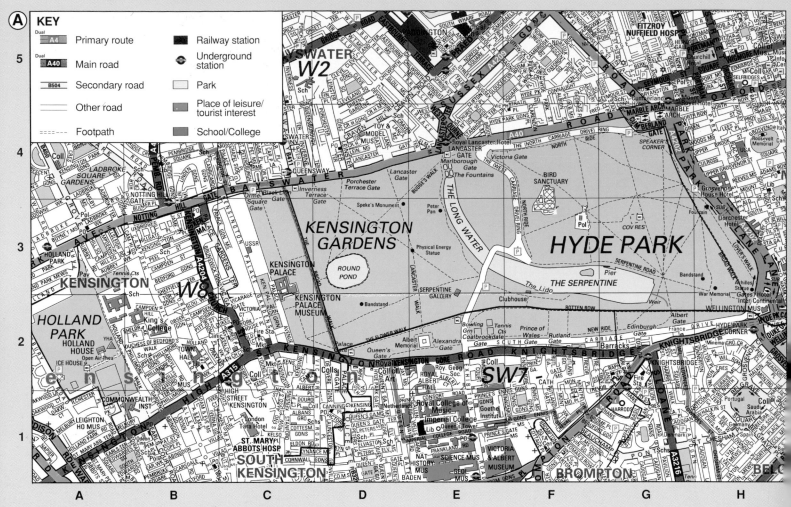

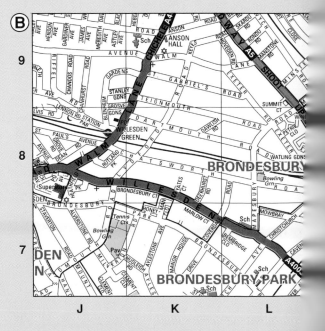

1 centimetre on the map measures 200 m on the ground

Maps can be used to help you plan journeys.

Maps **A** and **B** are **street maps**. You can use street maps to find your way around. Map **A** shows part of central London.

Map **C** is a **rail map** of the London Underground. It shows the order of the stations along the lines. This map can be used to plan a longer journey.

Map **D** is a **bus map**. It shows some of the bus routes in central London.

Street, rail and bus maps can be used together to plan a journey.

Anna and Tony are going to meet friends at The Commonwealth Institute in **B1** on map **A**.

They will go by Underground train from the statio near their home in Dartmouth Road in **K8** on ma **B**. They are then going into Hyde Park. Use the map to help plan their journey.

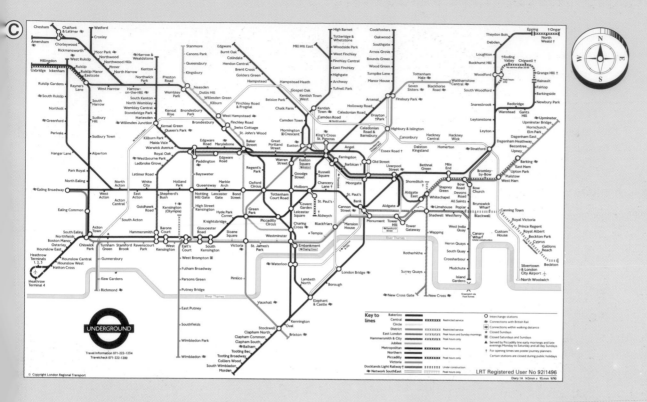

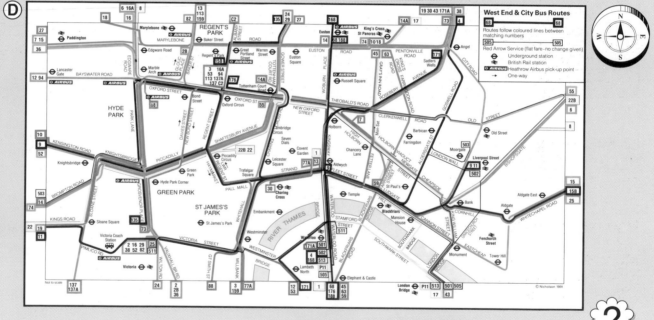

1 Which station is nearest Anna and Tony's home?

2 Which station is nearest to The Commonwealth Institute?

3 To get from home to The Commonwealth Institute Anna and Tony need to change Underground trains. Which station will they change at?
Which main road will Anna and Tony walk along from The Commonwealth Institute to Palace Gate to go into Hyde Park?

5 Anna and Tony see the statue of Peter Pan in Hyde Park. What is its grid reference?

6 Which direction would they go to see the Bird Sanctuary?

7 They walk across the grass to Speaker's Corner. About how far is it from the Bird Sanctuary?

8 Use map D. Which buses could Anna and Tony catch from Marble Arch to Baker Street station?

9 Use the maps to plan a journey to other places in central London for Anna and Tony.

Landshape - hills on maps

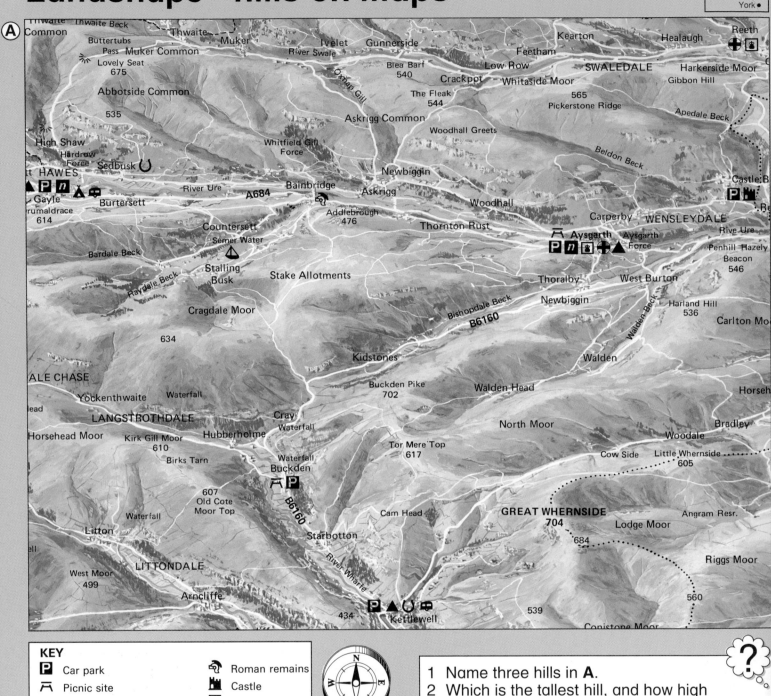

KEY

P	Car park	**🐎**	Roman remains
⊼	Picnic site	**🏰**	Castle
☀	Viewpoint	**🏛**	Museum
🚐	Touring caravan site	**⛵**	Sailing
⛺	Camping site	**U**	Horse riding / Trekking
▲	Youth hostel	**n**	National park centre
✚	Mountain rescue post	**.....**	National park boundary
- - -	Pennine Way	**546**	Heights in metres

A is an oblique aerial view of part of the Yorshire Dales National Park. In this **picture map** you can see rivers, lakes, roads, villages and many hills. It shows places where you can park, camp and visit. Many of the hills are high and steep sided. The number next to each hilltop tells you how high it is in metres.

1. Name three hills in **A**.
2. Which is the tallest hill, and how high is it?
3. How are woods shown in **A**?
4. Draw three symbols that show where you could stay for the night.
5. If you travelled from Aysgarth to Hawes which river would you see to the north of the road?
6. Would you walk uphill or downhill from Semer Water to the top of Cragdale Moor?
7. You are driven from Kettlewell to Aysgarth in a car. Describe what you would go past and where you would go up and down hill.

B is an old map. It was made by a famous mapmaker named John Speed in 1610. It shows most of the area that you can see in **A**. On his map, Speed showed the rivers and villages. The rivers are shown by lines and the villages by the symbol of a church. He also showed the land was hilly by drawing hill shapes as symbols on the map. These **hillocks** show where hills are. Find Penhill Beacon on **A** and **B**. Look for other places that are shown on both maps. For some you will find the spelling has changed.

Later mapmakers, like Christopher Greenwood, tried to show a clearer picture of the shape of the land by using symbols called **hachures**, which are short, thin lines drawn close together. Map **C**, printed in 1817, shows part of the same area as **B**. On it hachures are used to show which way and how much the land slopes. The hachures always point downhill. From them you can see where the land is higher or lower.

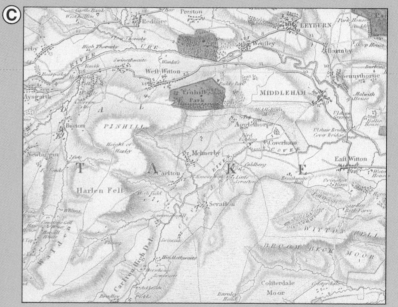

Present day mapmakers also want to show which way and how much the land slopes. Map **D** shows one way this is done. **Hill-shading** is used to show the shape and the slope of the land. Some of the hilltops are shown by a symbol, a name and a height in metres.

1 Name the rivers shown on map **C**.
2 Which of maps **B**, **C** and **D** is the oldest?
3 Name three features that appear on all three of maps **B**, **C** and **D**.
4 Which map do you think shows hills best?
5 Maps **B** and **C** do not have a key. Make a key for each of them.

KEY

Moorland	Farmland	═══ Main road
Forest and woodland	Town	─── Secondary road
▲487 Spot height in metres	─── Railway	═══ Other road

15

Landshape - showing height on maps

A

Neuadd Wen · Road · Pen-y-graig · Church · Hotel · Cartref · Gray Stones

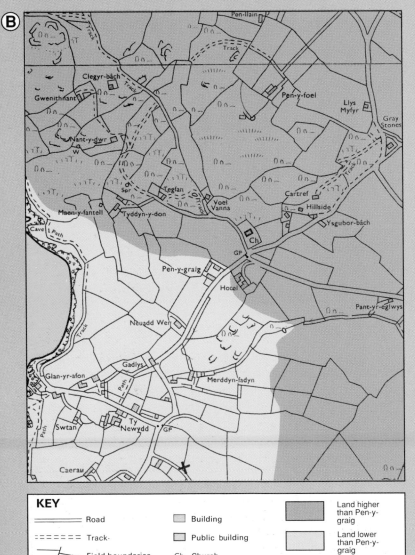

B

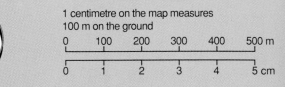

1 centimetre on the map measures
100 m on the ground

| 0 | 100 | 200 | 300 | 400 | 500 m |
| 0 | 1 | 2 | 3 | 4 | 5 cm |

Photo **A** shows a landscape in Anglesey, an island off the northwest coast of Wales. Some of the features have been named. One is the farm named Pen-y-graig.
You can see that the land is hilly. North of the farm is a hill with a stone barn on its top. To the north and east of the farm you can see the land is higher than the farm. To the southwest the land is lower. We can see the **slope** of the land.

B is a map of the area you can see in photo **A**. The red cross on map **B** marks the place where photo **A** was taken. Find Pen-y-graig on map **B**. Colours have been used on the map to show where the land is higher than the farm and where it is lower. A map that shows height like this is called a **layer-coloured map**.

1 Was photo **A** taken looking north, east, south or west?
2 Find the church. Is it on higher or lower ground than Pen-y-graig?
3 Name three places on lower ground than Pen-y-graig.
4 Is the feature coloured blue higher or lower than the land coloured green?
5 In which direction does the landscape in **A** and **B** slope?

KEY

———— Road	▢ Building	▭	Land higher than Pen-y-graig
======= Track	▢ Public building	▭	Land lower than Pen-y-graig
✗ Field boundaries	Ch Church	Direction of flow of water	
∩ ∩ ⌐ Scrub	GP Guide post	～～ Stream	
⑾⑾ Heath	Spr Spring		
Rock outcrop	W Well	▭	Water (Sea)

16

Landshape - contours

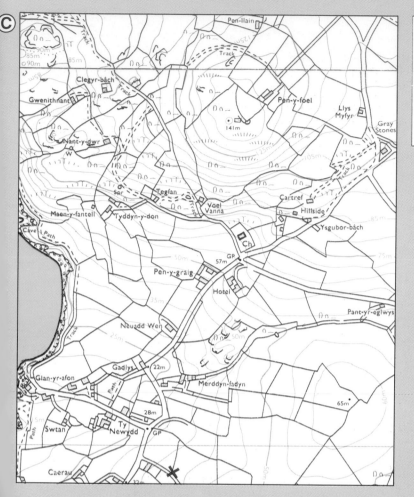

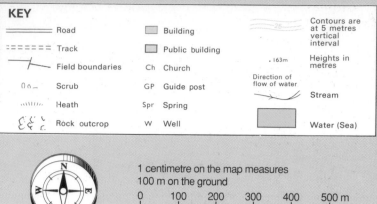

1 centimetre on the map measures
100 m on the ground

```
0     100    200    300    400    500 m
0      1      2      3      4      5 cm
```

From map **B** we can see that the land slopes, but it does not tell us how **high** the land is. To find this out we need to know the **height** of the land above sea level.

Map **C** shows the same area that you can see in map **B**. On map **C** the height of the land is shown by a dot with a number next to it, like this:

. 141m

This is called a **spot height**. It shows the spot where the land is 141 metres higher than sea level. Find spot height 141m. It marks the top of the hill you can see in photo **A**.

Another way to show the height of the land is by **contour lines**. You can see them on map **C**. They are the thin brown lines. A contour line shows that the land along it is all the same height above sea level. A number shows how high, in metres, the land along it is.

On map **C** you can see from the contour lines that the hill north of Pen-y-graig has a round **shape**. The contour lines show the shape and **slope** of the land. You can tell from them **which way** the land slopes. From the **height** of each contour line you can see **how much** the ground slopes. Contour lines close together mean a steep slope. Where they are far apart the slope is gentle.

1 Does spot height 65m mark a hilltop?
2 Write the height of the lowest spot height.
3 Find the hotel. What is the height of the contour line southwest of it?
4 Is the church on higher or lower ground than the hotel?

5 Is the slope to the north of the church gentle or steep?
6 You walk from the guide post near the church to Gray Stones house along the road. Do you go up or down hill? Say what you pass.

Decreasing scales - a local area

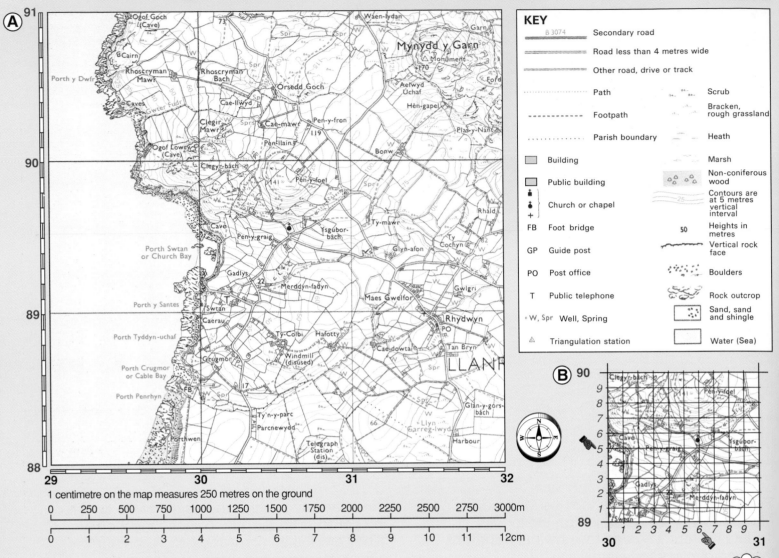

KEY

B 3074	Secondary road
	Road less than 4 metres wide
	Other road, drive or track
.... Path	Scrub
- - - - - - - Footpath	Bracken, rough grassland
.... Parish boundary	Heath
▢ Building	Marsh
▢ Public building	Non-coniferous wood
♦ Church or chapel	Contours are at 5 metres vertical interval
FB Foot bridge	50 Heights in metres
GP Guide post	Vertical rock face
PO Post office	Boulders
T Public telephone	Rock outcrop
W, Spr Well, Spring	Sand, sand and shingle
△ Triangulation station	Water (Sea)

1 centimetre on the map measures 250 metres on the ground

0   250   500   750   1000 1250 1500 1750 2000 2250 2500 2750 3000m

0   1   2   3   4   5   6   7   8   9   10   11   12cm

Map **A** shows more of the landscape of Anglesey around Pen-y-graig. The contour lines show how hilly the landscape is. Look carefully and you will see the shape of several hills. Spot heights mark the top of some of the hills.

Look for the church near Pen-y-graig. It is in grid square **30,89**. To say exactly where it is, it helps to give a grid reference that shows its site **inside** the grid square. To do this, we must imagine the grid square has been divided into one hundred smaller squares, like **B**. We can then work out the **six-figure grid reference** for the church by counting the tenths along the southern and western sides of the grid square. In **B** you can see that the church is on the sixth line east of grid line **30**, and nearest the fifth line north of grid line **89**. Its six-figure grid reference is **306,895**.

1 Give the six-figure grid reference for a spot height in grid square **30,89**.
2 Is there a hilltop at **314,897** or at **312,883**?
3 You are walking northwest along the footpath at **317,903**. Are you walking uphill or downhill?
4 Look at the coastline. Does the land slope steeply or gently to the sea?
5 How far is the church at **306,895** from the post office at Rhydwyn **315,889** in a straight line?
6 In which direction is the monument at **315,907** from Pen-y-graig **305,895**?
7 What feature do the contour lines show is between Caerau **302,889** and Rhydwyn **315,889**?
8 If you walked from Caerau to Rhydwyn along footpaths, name the places you would pass.

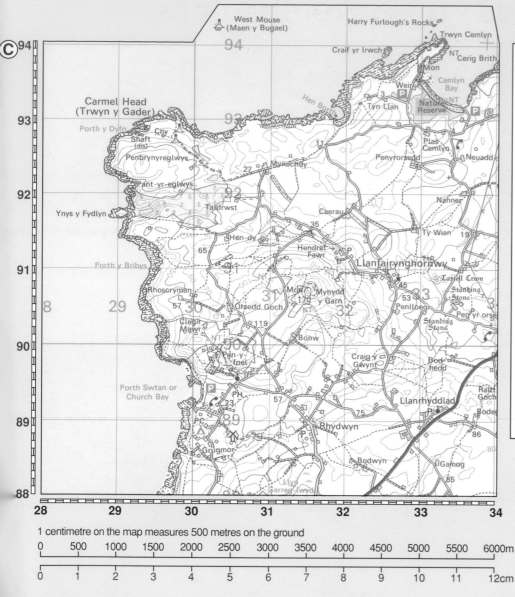

Map scale:

1 centimetre on the map measures 500 metres on the ground

0	500	1000	1500	2000	2500	3000	3500	4000	4500	5000	5500	6000m

0	1	2	3	4	5	6	7	8	9	10	11	12cm

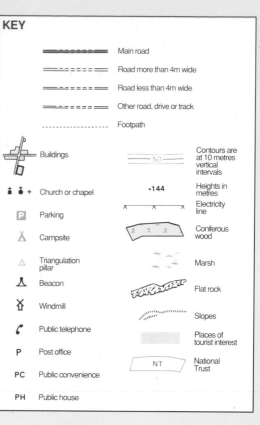

KEY

▬▬▬	Main road
═ ═ ═	Road more than 4m wide
─ ─ ─	Road less than 4m wide
─ ─ ─	Other road, drive or track
·········	Footpath
🏘	Buildings
♟ ♟ +	Church or chapel
P	Parking
⚑	Campsite
△	Triangulation pillar
⚲	Beacon
⚟	Windmill
✆	Public telephone
P	Post office
PC	Public convenience
PH	Public house
〜50〜	Contours are at 10 metres vertical intervals
•144	Heights in metres
⋊⋉	Electricity line
🌲	Coniferous wood
⋮⋮	Marsh
〰	Flat rock
▪▪▪	Slopes
▨	Places of tourist interest
NT	National Trust

D

Name	Meaning
craig	crag
hen	old
mynydd	mountain
pant	hollow
pen	hill
porth	bay
rhyd	ford
ty	house
y	of the
ynys	island

Map **C** shows a larger area of Anglesey. Pen-y-graig is not named on this map, but it is marked at grid reference **305,895**, just southwest of the church.

The contour lines on map **C** show that the land is very hilly. Along the coast the symbols show that is rocky. Look at grid square **32,93**. You can see the hachure lines pointing downhill to the rocks. They show that the coast is very steep and that probably there are cliffs there. Use the key to see what other features are shown on the map.

In the south of map **C** you can see the village of Rhydwyn. There are two other small villages shown on the map: Llanfairynghornwy and Llanrhyddlad. Both names start with 'llan' which means church in Welsh. You can see churches in both villages. **D** shows what some of the other names on the map mean.

1 Find the names of three hills or mountains on map **C**.
2 Why would you expect to find a stream going through the village of Rhydwyn?
3 What symbol shows that there is probably a wood in grid squares **29,91** and **30,91**?
4 Find the church at **332,891**. Imagine you are looking northeast along the main road. Is the road sloping uphill or downhill?
5 Give the six-figure grid reference for a place where you could camp. What other facilities could you use there?

19

Decreasing scales - towns and regions

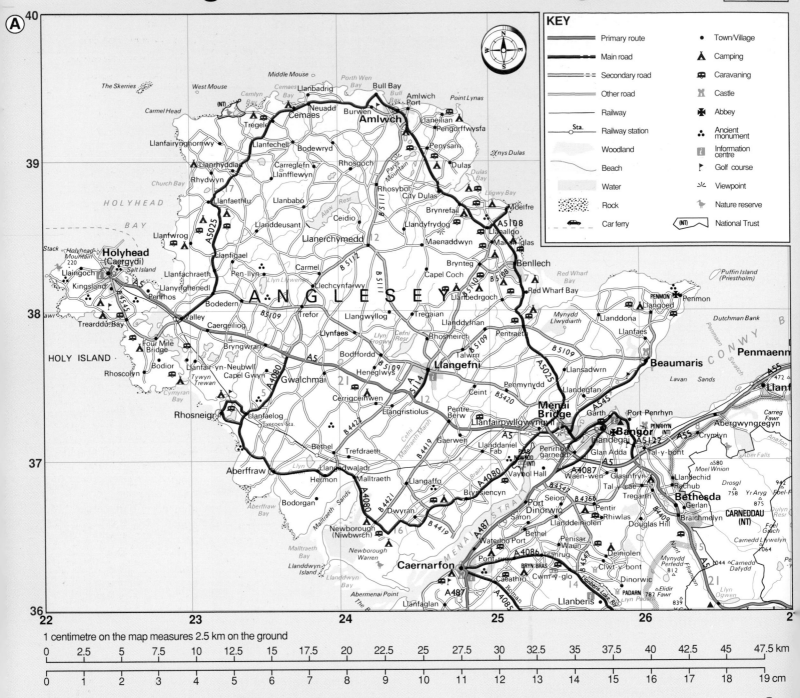

1 centimetre on the map measures 2.5 km on the ground

Map **A** shows the whole of Anglesey. It is drawn to a smaller scale than the map on page 19. You can see that Anglesey is an island. It is off the northwest coast of Wales. The towns of Bangor and Caernarfon are on the mainland.

Find the villages of Rhydwyn, Llanrhyddlad and Llanfairynghornwy in the northwest of Anglesey. You can see that there are many villages and towns on Anglesey. Map **A** shows you that there are many places where people go camping and can stay in caravans. It also shows places like nature reserves, which people like to visit.

1 On which side of Anglesey are there most camping and caravan sites?
2 Find the railway line on map **A**. At which town west of Anglesey does it end? Why?
3 Which main road would you drive along from Holyhead to Menai Bridge?
4 In which towns could you visit an Information Centre to find out about what to visit on Anglesey?
5 Draw symbols to show three places you could visit on a day out on Anglesey.

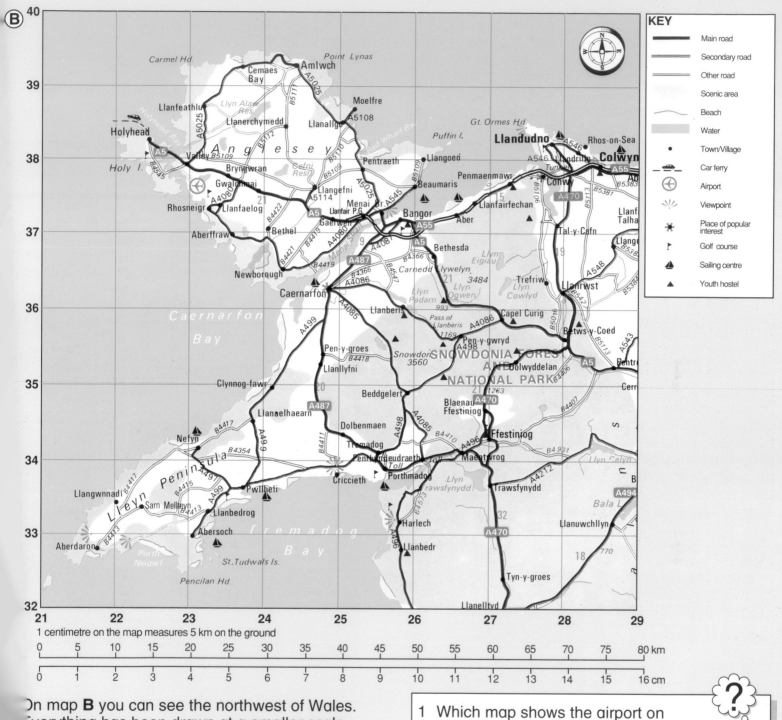

KEY

▬▬▬	Main road
═══	Secondary road
───	Other road
	Scenic area
~~	Beach
	Water
•	Town/Village
🚗	Car ferry
✈	Airport
☀	Viewpoint
✳	Place of popular interest
⚑	Golf course
⛵	Sailing centre
▲	Youth hostel

1 centimetre on the map measures 5 km on the ground

0 5 10 15 20 25 30 35 40 45 50 55 60 65 70 75 80 km

0 1 2 3 4 5 6 7 8 9 10 11 12 13 14 15 16 cm

On map **B** you can see the northwest of Wales. Everything has been drawn at a smaller scale than on map **A**. Many places have been left off.

Map **B** is a **route planning map** for drivers to use. It shows the main roads and some of the minor roads. It can be used by drivers to plan the main part of their journeys.

Map **A** shows many more roads than map **B**. There are other features that **A** shows which **B** does not, such as the railway to Holyhead. Maps of the same area do not always show the same things.

1 Which map shows the airport on Anglesey?
2 What activities do maps **A** and **B** show you could do at Caenarfon?
3 Imagine you are staying at Bets-y-Coed, in grid square **28,35** on map **B**. Use maps **A** and **B** to help you plan a car journey so that you can visit these places during the day: Beaumaris Castle, the Information Centre in Caernarfon and the nature reserve at grid reference **233,394** on map **A**. List in order the roads used and places visited.

The shape of the Earth

One of the best known photos of Earth was taken from the spacecraft Apollo 11 on its way to the Moon in July 1969. It shows the Earth as a ball in space. You can see that **space photo** in **A**.

More than two thousand years ago some people, like the Greeks Aristotle and Eratosthenes, had worked out that the Earth is a sphere, shaped like a ball. But it was not until an expedition led by the Portuguese sailor Ferdinand Magellan sailed round the world between 1519 and 1522 that it was proved that the Earth is round.

It was only in the 1960s that photographs, like **A**, from space showed that the Earth is a sphere. The first people to see this view of the Earth were the astronauts on Apollo 8, when they orbited the Moon over Christmas 1968.

In 150 AD the Greek astronomer Ptolomy described how to model the Earth as a **globe**. Yet it is only in the last few hundred years that accurate globes have been made.

A globe, like the one in **B**, is the only way to show the shape of all the features on the Earth accurately. A globe also shows the proper positions of the continents and oceans. And it shows how large they are compared to each other.

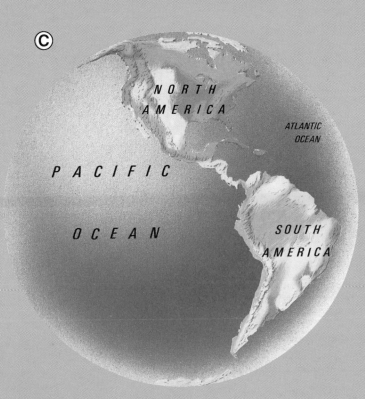

Drawings, like **C**, are another way to show a view of the Earth as though it is a sphere seen from space.

1 Which continents and oceans are shown in **A** and **B**?
2 Why can you not see all the continents and oceans in photo **A**?
3 Which continents and oceans are shown in drawing **C**?

A **map** of the Earth has to show the whole of a sphere on flat paper. Because maps are flat, they do not show the Earth's curved shape completely accurately. This can only be done by changing the exact shape and size of the continents and oceans either slightly or quite a lot.

Map **D** is a **world map**. It shows one way to draw the continents and oceans. It shows **where** they are. Their shapes, sizes and positions look very like they do on a globe.

Maps **E** and **F** show other ways to draw the shape of the Earth on flat paper. We can recognise the continents and oceans, but these maps change either the shape or the size of them.

World maps also make it look as though the Earth has edges! We have to remember that the ocean on the left of the map is part of the ocean on the right of the map.

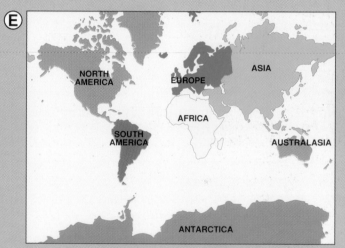

Mercator's map shows directions correctly, but not the sizes of continents.

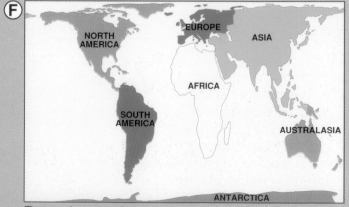

Peters' map shows sizes correctly, but not the shape of the continents.

?

1 Which ocean is shown on both the left and the right of the map?
2 What differences can you spot in the way the Earth is shown on maps **D**, **E** and **F**?
3 Why is a globe a more accurate way to show the Earth than a flat map?

Where on Earth are we? - Latitude and Longitude

It has always been important for us to know where we are. For sailors, like Ferdinand Magellan, it has been even more important to have a system of finding out where they are on the oceans, so they know how far they are from land and can work out when they might reach it.

To help them work out their **position**, sailors use a system of grid lines. These are imaginary lines drawn around the globe.
These lines are called lines of **latitude** and **longitude**. They are used to work out a grid reference which tells you your position on land and at sea.

Lines of latitude are lines which run in an east-west direction around the Earth. They are drawn in blue on **A**. The most important line of latitude is the **Equator**, which goes round the middle of the world. Find it on **A**.

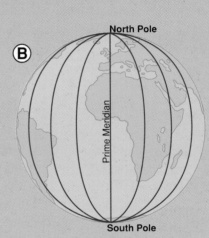

Lines of longitude are lines which run from the North Pole to the South Pole. They are drawn in red on **B**. The most important line of longitude is called the **Prime Meridian**. Find it on **B**.

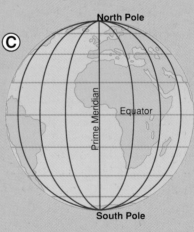

C shows the lines of latitude and longitude as they would appear on a globe. They can also be drawn on world maps. **D** shows how these grid lines appear on a map of the world.

1. Is the equator a line of latitude or longitude?
2. Where is the Prime Meridian drawn from and to?
3. How would the lines of latitude and longitude help a lone sailor on a voyage round the world?

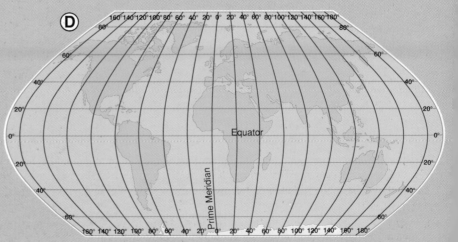

24

give grid references using latitude and
ngitude, the grid lines must be numbered.
ach of the lines of latitude and longitude
e numbered in **degrees**.

he **lines of latitude** are numbered from the
quator. The Equator is given the number 0 .
he lines of latitude **north** of the Equator
e given a **number** and the **letter N**. So the
e of latitude 20° north of the equator is
elled 20°N. The lines of latitude south
the equator are numbered and lettered **S**.

The **lines of longitude** are numbered from the
Prime Meridian. The Prime Meridian is given the
number 0 . The lines of longitude **west** of the
Prime Meridian are given a **number** and the **letter
W**. So, the line of longitude 60° west of the Prime
Meridian is labelled 60°W. The lines of longitude
east of the Prime Meridian are numbered and
lettered **E**.

To find a grid reference you have to use the lines
of latitude and longitude together.
The line of latitude is written first, then the line of
longitude.

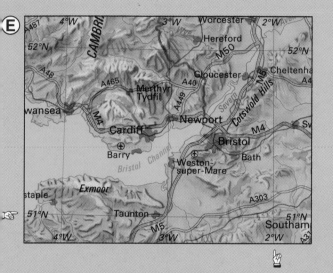

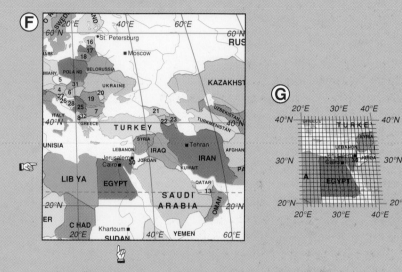

ok at **E**. It shows an area from map **A** on pages
-31. The lines of latitude and longitude are
own at 1° intervals.
find Bristol on **E** you must:
ut your finger on 51°N at the side of **E**
ut your finger on 2°W at the bottom of **E**
ove both fingers along the grid lines until they
eet.
istol is in the grid square to the north and west.
grid reference is 51°N 2°W.

F shows an area from map **A** on pages 42-43.
It shows only some lines of latitude and longitude.
It cannot show every line so it gives lines at
intervals of 20° as a guide. We have to estimate
the lines of latitude and longitude in between by
imagining that these lines are drawn in, like
diagram **G**.
On **F** you can see that Cairo is north of 20°N and
east of 20°E. To give a more exact reference to
the nearest degree we must count the lines north
of 20°N and east of 20°E. Cairo is on the 10th line
north of 20°N so it is at 30°N. It is on the 11th line
east of 20°E so it is at 31°E. Therefore its grid
reference is 30°N 31°E.

You can use latitude and longitude to help you find
places in an atlas. The Index on pages 46-47
gives latitude and longitude references to places
found on the maps on pages 28-31 and 40-45.

> **?**
> Use map **E**. What is the reference for
> Cardiff?
> On map **E**, what is the reference for
> Gloucester?
> Use map **F**. What is the reference for Tehran?
> On map **F**, what is the reference for
> Khartoum?
> On map **F**, what is the reference for Moscow?

Introducing atlas maps

The **key** tells you what the symbols on the map mean. You can find out more about them on pages 28-29.

The **scale bar** is used to measure distances on the map.

The **compass** is used to work out directions on the map.

The **title** names the map. You will find it listed on the contents page of this book.

The lines of latitude and longitude help you to give **grid references** to say where places are on the map. Use the **index** on pages 46-47 to help you find places.

The **page number** helps you to find where the maps are in the book. Use the **contents** page and the **index** to help you.

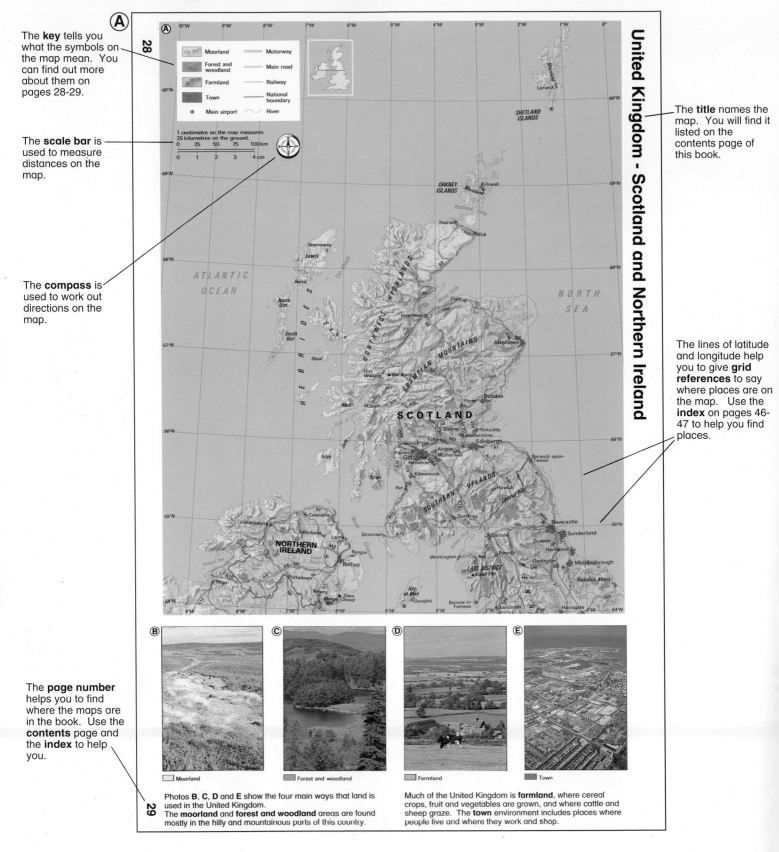

United Kingdom - Scotland and Northern Ireland

Photos **B**, **C**, **D** and **E** show the four main ways that land is used in the United Kingdom.
The **moorland** and **forest and woodland** areas are found mostly in the hilly and mountainous parts of this country.

Much of the United Kingdom is **farmland**, where cereal crops, fruit and vegetables are grown, and where cattle and sheep graze. The **town** environment includes places where people live and where they work and shop.

The maps you will explore on the following pages show the British Isles, Europe and the World.

A shows you two pages 28-29 that have been reduced. The notes around the outside of **A** tell you what to use to understand the maps on the following pages.

Some of the maps are drawn like map **A** to show how the land is used. They are called **environment maps.** You can find out more about them on pages 28-29 and 30-31.

Environment maps are one type of **thematic map. B** shows a thematic map from page 32 of this book. Thematic maps are drawn to show information about a special topic or theme. This is done to make it easier for you to find out about that topic from the map.

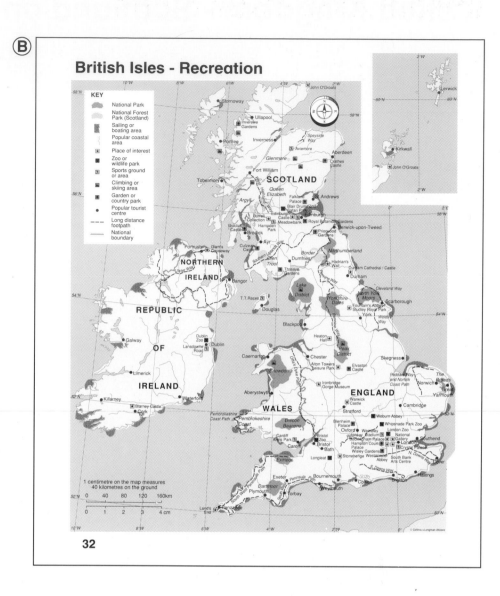

B

British Isles - Recreation

32

C

C is part of a thematic map on page 41, which shows the position and shape of the countries in Europe.

It is important to remember that every map shows only selected information about a place or part of the World, whether it is a map of a town, a country, or the World.

?

1 What is the title of map **B**?
2 Is map **A** drawn with south at the top or the bottom of the map?
3 What do you think the title for map **C** should be?
4 What are the grid references on map **A** for Inverness and Belfast?
5 Why is map **B** called a thematic map?

Mainland
Lerwick
SHETLAND ISLANDS

NORTH SEA

Kirkwall
Mainland
ORKNEY ISLANDS
Pentland Firth
Thurso
Wick
A882
A9

Aberdeen
A96
A94
Dundee
Perth
A95
GRAMPIAN MOUNTAINS
Elgin
Moray Firth
A96
A9
Inverness
A9
A82
Loch Ness
HIGHLANDS
NORTHWEST
Ben Nevis
Fort William
A82
A828
A85

THE MINCH
Stornoway
Lewis
Harris
SKYE
Rhum
HEBRIDES
North Uist
South Uist

ATLANTIC OCEAN

Legend

Moorland	Motorway
Forest and woodland	Main road
Farmland	Railway
Town	National boundary
⊕ Main airport	River

1 centimetre on the map measures
25 kilometres on the ground.

0 25 50 75 100km

0 1 2 3 4 cm

N E S W

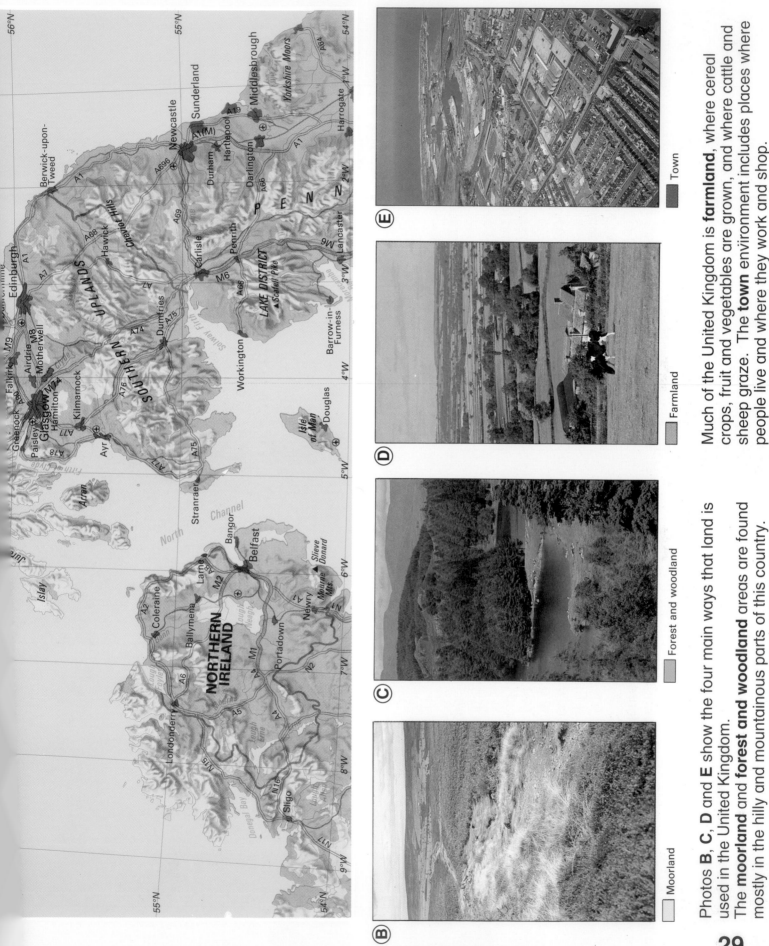

Moorland

(B)

Forest and woodland

(C)

Farmland

(D)

Town

(E)

Photos **B**, **C**, **D** and **E** show the four main ways that land is used in the United Kingdom.
The **moorland** and **forest and woodland** areas are found mostly in the hilly and mountainous parts of this country.

Much of the United Kingdom is **farmland**, where cereal crops, fruit and vegetables are grown, and where cattle and sheep graze. The **town** environment includes places where people live and work and shop.

29

United Kingdom - England and Wales

A is an environmental map of two of the countries in the United Kingdom. Look at the key. It tells you what the different environments shown on the map are.

Find Dartmoor in southwest England. It is in grid square 50°N 3°W. See how it is coloured. The key tells us that Dartmoor is moorland.

Find Manchester in northwest England. It is in grid square 53°N 2°W. The red colour shows that it has a town environment. There are many buildings there, where people live, work and shop. You can see the environment around Manchester is farmland and moorland.

Look at other parts of England and Wales to see what types of environment there are.

1 Find grid square 52°N 1°E. Name the city which has an airport near it.

2 Find Newcastle in grid square 54°N 1°W. What type of environment is it?

3 Find Anglesey in grid square 53°N 4°W. What type of environment covers the island?

4 Find grid square 51°N 3°W. Name a town in the grid square. What other environments can you see in the square?

5 Name a grid square which shows only farmland and town environments.

6 Name a grid square which shows a large area of moorland and woodland and forest.

7 Which type of environment covers most of England and Wales?

8 Is there more town environment in England or Wales?

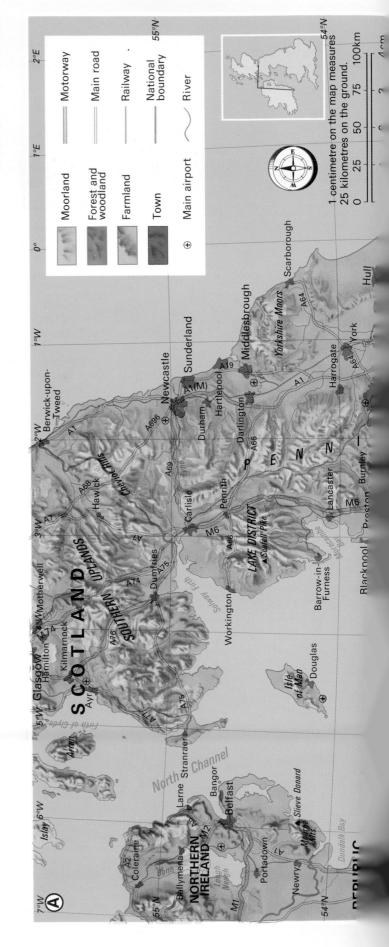

NORTH SEA

ENGLAND

WALES

CAMBRIAN MOUNTAINS

IRELAND

FRANCE

English Channel

St. George's Channel

Bristol Channel

Cardigan Bay

Isle of Wight

Channel Islands (U.K.)

Grimsby
Doncaster
Rotherham
Barnsley M18
M1
Sheffield
Manchester
Stockport
Widnes
Warrington
M56
Ellesmere Port
Macclesfield
M6
Liverpool
Birkenhead
M53
Rhyl
Chester
Crewe
Stoke
Stafford
Telford
Shrewsbury
Wrexham
Colwyn Bay
Bangor
Anglesey
Snowdon A5
A5
A487
Aberystwyth
Milford Haven
Swansea
A40
A465
Merthyr Tydfil
Cardiff
Barry
Newport
A449
Weston-super-Mare
Gloucester
Cheltenham
A40
Hereford
Worcester
Kidderminster
Wolverhampton
Walsall
Birmingham
Solihull
M5
M6
Coventry
Rugby
Royal Leamington Spa
Nuneaton
M1
Leicester
Derby
Burton upon Trent
A38
Nottingham
Mansfield
Lincoln
Boston
The Wash
The Fens
Peterborough
A1
Corby
A604
Northampton
Milton Keynes
Bedford
Cambridge
Norwich
Lowestoft
Ipswich
A11
A12
Colchester
Stevenage
M11
Harlow
Chelmsford
Luton
St. Albans
A1(M)
Watford
M25
Basildon
Southend
Gillingham
Ramsgate
Dover
Folkestone
M2
Maidstone
M20
A21
Hastings
Eastbourne
Bognor Regis
Brighton
M23
A23
Crawley
Aldershot
Woking
A3
M3
Basingstoke
Reading
M4
Swindon
Oxford
M40
Slough
London
Chiltern Hills
Milton Keynes
South Downs
M27
Portsmouth
Southampton
A31
A27
Bournemouth
Weymouth
Cotswold Hills
Bristol
Bath
A303
M5
Newport
Barry
Taunton
Exmoor
A38
Barnstaple
A30
Exeter
Torbay
Dartmoor
Plymouth
A30
Falmouth
Penzance
Isles of Scilly
Severn
Avon
Thames
Trent
Ouse
Nene
Avon
Wye
Calais
Boulogne
Dieppe
Le Havre
Rouen
Cherbourg
Caen
Guernsey
St. Peter Port
Jersey
St. Helier
N1
N28
A13
N15
A13
N13
N13
N15
Channel Tunnel
St. of Dover

Wexford
Dublin
N1
N11
N11
Slaney

31

British Isles - Recreation

KEY

- National Park
- National Forest Park (Scotland)
- Sailing or boating area
- Popular coastal area
- ★ Place of interest
- Zoo or wildlife park
- Sports ground or area
- Climbing or skiing area
- Garden or country park
- Popular tourist centre
- Long distance footpath
- National boundary

John O'Groats

Stornoway

Ullapool

Inverewe Gardens

Portree

Inverness

Aviemore

Aberdeen

Glenmore

Crathes Castle

Tobermory

Fort William

SCOTLAND

West Highland Way

Queen Elizabeth

Falkland Palace

St.Andrews

Argyll

Blair Drummond Safari Park

Burrell Collection

Edinburgh

Edinburgh

Royal Botanical Gardens

Brodick Castle

Meadowbank

Hampden Park

Priorwood Gardens

Berwick-upon-Tweed

Brodick

Culzean Castle

Ayr

Southern Uplands Way

Glen Trool

Border

Northumberland

Dumfries

Hadrian's Wall

Durham Cathedral / Castle

Portrush

Giant's Causeway

Threave Gardens

Pennine Way

Durham

NORTHERN

IRELAND

Ulster Way

Cleveland Way

Lake District

North York Moors

Bangor

T.T.Races

Yorkshire Dales

Scarborough

REPUBLIC

Douglas

Fountain's Abbey Studley Royal Park

York

Wolds Way

Galway

Blackpool

Heaton Hall

Pennine Way

Peak District

OF

Dublin Zoo

Dublin

Caernarfon

Chester

Skegness

Lansdowne Road

Snowdonia

Offa's Dyke Path

Alton Towers Leisure Park

Elvaston Castle

Limerick

IRELAND

Aberystwyth

Ironbridge Gorge Museum

Peddars Way and Norfolk Coast Path

Norwich

The Broads

ENGLAND

Gre Yarmou

Killarney

Blarney Castle

Cork

Waterford

WALES

Warwick Castle

Stratford

Cambridge

Pembrokeshire Coast Path

Pembrokeshire Coast

Brecon Beacons

Woburn Abbey

Blenheim Palace

Whipsnade Park Zoo

Oxford

Wembley Stadium

London Zoo

National Gallery

London

Southend

Cardiff Arms Park

Bristol Zoo

Ridgeway

Buckingham Palace

Hampton Court Palace

Crystal Palace

Cardiff

Bristol

Bath

Wisley Gardens

Stonehenge

Westminster Abbey

South Bank Arts Centre

N. Downs Way

Exmoor

Longleat

S. Downs Way

Dover

Dartmoor

Exeter

Peninsula Path

Bournemouth

Cowes

Weymouth

Brighton

Hastings

Plymouth

Torbay

South West Peninsula Path

Land's End

Penzance

1 centimetre on the map measures
40 kilometres on the ground

| 0 | 40 | 80 | 120 | 160km |

| 0 | 1 | 2 | 3 | 4 cm |

Lerwick

Kirkwall

John O'Groats

© Collins<>Longman Atlas

Map **A** is a thematic map which shows some of the places in the British Isles where people go for a day out or for a holiday. Use the key to see what sort of places can be visited.

Maps **B** and **C** show two places which people often visit: the seaside resort of Blackpool and Exmoor National Park. Use the keys to see what each map shows.

1 Which map is a street map?
2 Name three things a holiday-maker could do in Blackpool.
3 Give the grid references for three places of historic interest in Exmoor National Park.
4 Name a place where people could visit to take part in an activity. Say what the activity is.

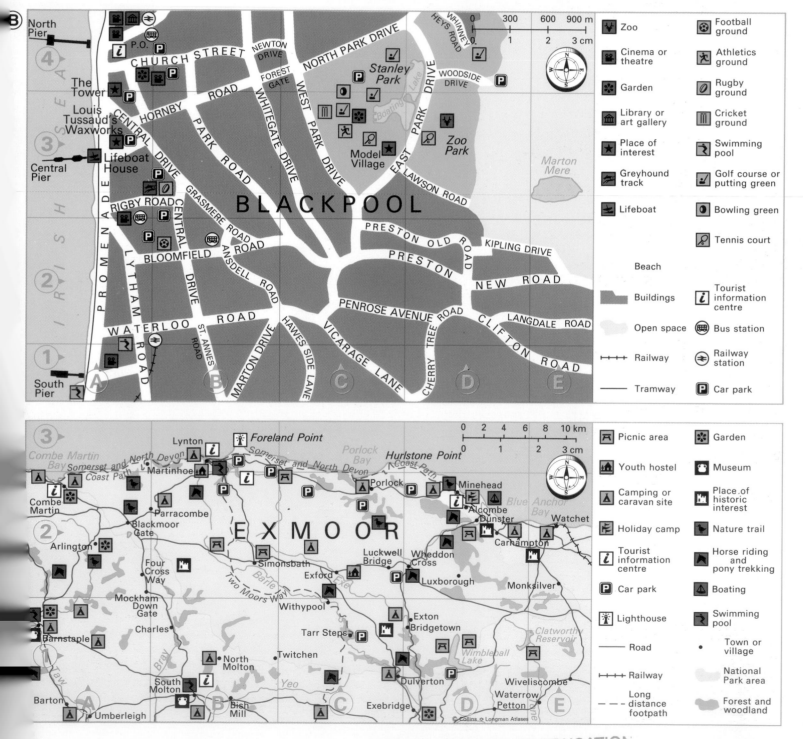

British Isles - Population

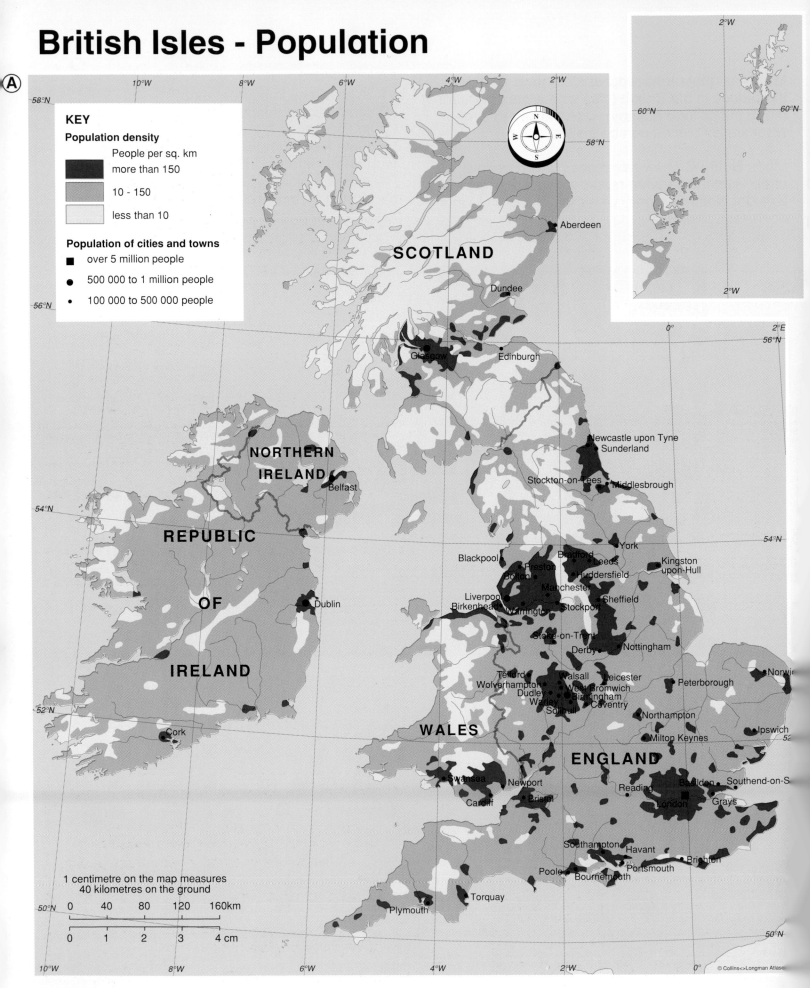

KEY

Population density

People per sq. km

more than 150

10 - 150

less than 10

Population of cities and towns

■ over 5 million people

● 500 000 to 1 million people

• 100 000 to 500 000 people

SCOTLAND

Aberdeen

Dundee

Glasgow

Edinburgh

NORTHERN IRELAND

Belfast

REPUBLIC

OF

IRELAND

Dublin

Cork

Newcastle upon Tyne

Sunderland

Stockton-on-Tees

Middlesbrough

York

Blackpool

Bradford

Leeds

Kingston upon-Hull

Preston

Huddersfield

Bolton

Manchester

Sheffield

Liverpool

Birkenhead

Warrington

Stockport

Stoke-on-Trent

Derby

Nottingham

Telford

Walsall

Leicester

Norwich

Wolverhampton

Peterborough

Dudley

West Bromwich

Warley

Birmingham

Coventry

Solihull

Northampton

Ipswich

WALES

Milton Keynes

ENGLAND

Swansea

Newport

Reading

Basildon

Southend-on-S

Cardiff

Bristol

London

Grays

Southampton

Havant

Brighton

Poole

Portsmouth

Bournemouth

Torquay

Plymouth

1 centimetre on the map measures
40 kilometres on the ground

0   40   80   120   160km

0   1   2   3   4 cm

© Collins<>Longman Atlases

Map **A** is a **population map**. The **population** is the number of people who live in a place. Some people live in the middle of large cities, like the part of central London you can see in photo **B**. Many people live in towns or the suburbs of cities, like Warwick in **C**. In **urban areas** like these, usually more than 150 people live on each square kilometre of land. They are very built up.

Fewer people live in villages and the countryside. Some villages have quite a lot of people living in them, like Abergynolwyn in Wales in **D**. In areas where most of the land is farmland homes are scattered about the countryside, like the farms in Hereford and Worcester in **E**. In these **rural areas** between 10 and 150 people live on each square kilometre of land.

Ⓑ

Ⓒ

In some rural areas, very few people live. In mountainous and moorland areas fewer than 10 people usually live on each square kilometre of land. Homes are few and far between, just as in the Lake District in Cumbria in photo **F**.

The key for map **A** shows that the colours on the map tell you where many or few people live in the British Isles. The map shows you roughly how many people live in the largest cities and towns. Map **A** is a thematic map.

1 Which city has over 5 million people living in it?
2 Name a part of the British Isles where few people live in each square kilometre.
3 Name five towns in areas where many people live.
4 Why do you think few people live in central Wales?
5 Do you think more people live on the Isle of Wight or the Isle of Man? Why?

Weather maps

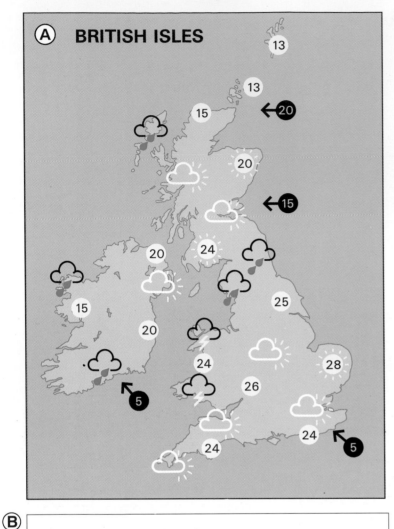

A BRITISH ISLES

Everyday we can see the **weather forecast** on television. On map **A** symbols are used to show what the weather may be like in each part of the British Isles. The key shows what the symbols mean. **B** is the weather forecast as it was printed in the paper. Satellite photo **C** shows how cloudy it was on the day the forecast was made.

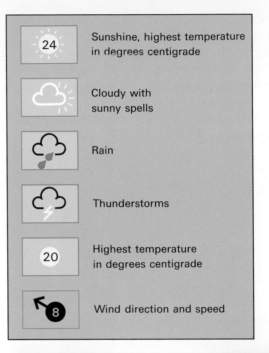

24	Sunshine, highest temperature in degrees centigrade
☁	Cloudy with sunny spells
☔	Rain
⛈	Thunderstorms
20	Highest temperature in degrees centigrade
↖8	Wind direction and speed

B

WEATHER

London, SE, central S, E, NW, central N, NE England, East Anglia, E, W Midlands, N Wales, Lake District: A few sunny intervals but thundery showers at times; wind SE light; max temp 25°C (77°F).

Channel Islands, SW England, S Wales: Sunny intervals, scattered showers developing, perhaps thundery; wind mainly SE light; max temp 22°C (72°F).

Isle of Man, SW Scotland, Glasgow, central Highlands, Moray Firth, Argyll, Northern Ireland: Some sunny intervals, isolated thundery showers; wind mainly E light; max temp 24°C (75°F).

Borders, Edinburgh, Dundee, Aberdeen: Mainly cloudy but a few sunny intervals developing away from coasts; wind E moderate; max temp 19°C (66°F).

NE, NW Scotland, Orkney, Shetland: Rather cloudy with outbreaks of rain and drizzle in places; wind E moderate; max temp 18°C (64°F).

Outlook for tomorrow and Saturday: Unsettled, with thundery showers in most areas, but also some sunny intervals; remaining very warm in sunnier areas.

1 How does **A** show hot or cold weather?
2 What was the weather forecast for Scotland?
3 Is the newspaper forecast for Wales in **B** the same as the weather forecast in **A**?
4 Which part of England does photo **C** show has no cloud?

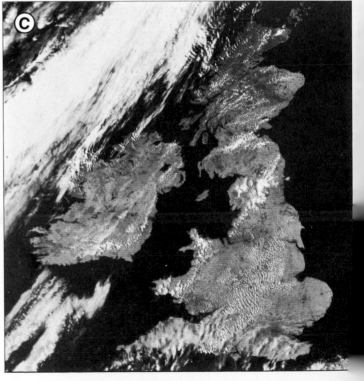

C

D EUROPE

(weather map)

8
10
8
12
20
26
24
29
28
30
28
32
28
29
30
32
32

E EUROPE

		C	F
Amsterdam	s	27	81
Athens	s	31	88
Barcelona	f	28	82
Belgrade	f	29	84
Berlin	s	28	82
Biarritz	c	29	84
Boulogne	c	24	75
Bordeaux	s	27	81
Brussels	s	25	77
Budapest	f	30	86
Cologne	s	27	81
Copenhagen	s	23	73
Dublin	c	18	64
Dubrovnik	s	25	77
Florence	c	29	84
Frankfurt	s	28	82
Geneva	f	26	79
Helsinki	f	18	64
Innsbruck	c	25	77
Lisbon	c	28	82
Locarno	c	26	79
Luxemburg	s	28	82
Madrid	c	30	86
Majorca	f	28	82
Malaga	s	30	86
Milan	s	29	84
Moscow	s	30	86
Munich	f	26	79
Naples	c	27	81
Nice	s	30	86
Oslo	c	18	64
Paris	s	24	75
Prague	s	28	82
Reykjavik	c	11	52
Rome	c	27	81
Salzburg	s	28	82
Stockholm	s	21	70
Strasbourg	s	28	82
Venice	s	30	86
Vienna	s	28	82
Warsaw	s	29	84

F

During the summer many people go to Europe for their holidays. Weather forecasters use a map like **D** to show what the weather may be like over the whole of the continent. Chart **E** shows the summer temperatures of some of the main resorts which people visit in Europe. **F** is a satellite photo which shows what the weather across Europe was actually like on the day for which the weather forecast was made.

?

Use the map of Europe on page 41 to help you with these questions.
1 Name the countries in Europe which photo **F** shows were cloudy.
2 Name three countries which had a clear, sunny day.
3 In which country is the hottest resort in **E**? Was the forecast for that part of Europe accurate or inaccurate?

British Isles

A is a satellite photo of the British Isles. The seas around the British Isles have been named on photo A. Some of the mountain areas on the islands of Britain and Ireland have been labelled too.

Map B show the British Isles. It tells us more about the land than the photo does. It shows more clearly where the high land is and where the low land is in Britain and Ireland. Colours are used to show the height of the land above sea level. It is a layer coloured map.

This type of map is called a **physical map**, because it shows the physical features of the islands. The physical features include the mountains, rivers, lowlands, moors, seas and islands.

Map B also shows where the countries in the British Isles are. It shows some of the towns as well.

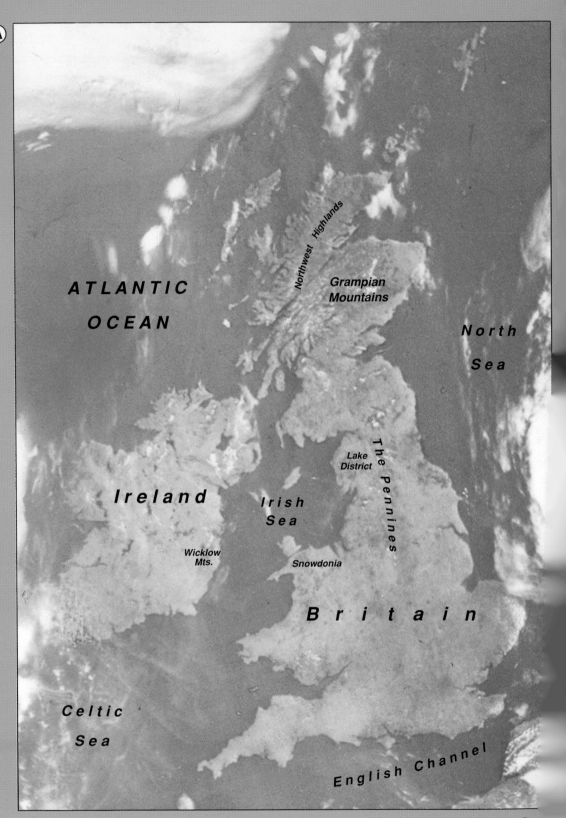

A

Northwest Highlands

Grampian Mountains

ATLANTIC OCEAN

North Sea

Ireland

Lake District

The Pennines

Irish Sea

Wicklow Mts.

Snowdonia

Britain

Celtic Sea

English Channel

---

1 Which mountains are named in Ireland on **A** and **B**?
2 Use the key. Which colour shows the highest land.
3 How are rivers shown on map **B**?

4 Which islands lie off northwest Scotland?
5 Say where the Isle of Man is.
6 Which moors are in southwest England?
7 What can you find out from map **B** which satellite photo **A** does not show?

B

60°N
12°W

1 centimetre on the map measures
50 kilometres on the ground

0   50   100   150   200 km

0   1   2   3   4 cm

10°W   8°W   6°W   4°W   2°W   0°   2°E

60°N

KEY

The colours show the height
of the land above sea level

Over 1000 metres
500 - 1000 metres
200 -500 metres
100 - 200 metres
0 - 100 metres

~~~ River

Lake

National boundary

■ Capital city

• Other city

Shetland
Islands

2°W

Orkney
Islands

58°N

Hebrides

Northwest Highlands

ATLANTIC

OCEAN

Grampian
Mountains

SCOTLAND

North

56°N

• Glasgow   ■ Edinburgh

Southern
Uplands

Sea

58°N

56°N

Tyne   • Newcastle
          upon Tyne

**NORTHERN
IRELAND**   ■ Belfast

U N I T E D

Lake
District

The Pennines

Ouse

54°N

REPUBLIC

OF

IRELAND

Isle of
Man

Irish Sea

K I N G D O M

■ Dublin

Anglesey

• Leeds

• Manchester
Liverpool •

Snowdonia

Trent

Wicklow
Mts.

Severn

• Birmingham

E N G L A N D

52°N

WALES

Thames

Cardiff ■   • Bristol   ■ London

Exmoor

• Southampton

Celtic
Sea

Dartmoor

Isle of Wight

E n g l i s h   C h a n n e l

50°N

10°W   8°W   Isles of   6°W   4°W   2°W   0°   2°E
                      Scilly

54°N

52°N

50°N

39

Europe

A

ATLANTIC OCEAN

Ireland

Britain

NORTH SEA

Rhine

Alps

Danube

MEDITERRANEAN SEA

A is a satellite photo of part of the continent of Europe. From the photo we can see the shape of the land and where the seas are. Some of the features have been named on photo **A**. But photo **A** does not show where the countries in Europe are.

On a map, the **boundaries** of the countries can be drawn. Map **B** is a thematic map which shows each country in Europe. It is a **political map**. It shows the **capital** city of each country. The capital city is where the government of a country meets. It shows some other important cities too.

Map **B** also shows where some of the rivers are in Europe.

1 Name the two countries which border Spain.
2 Which countries have borders with Germany?
3 Name the country which has borders with Belgium, Germany and France.
4 Which country has the Mediterranean Sea to its south and the Bay of Biscay to its west?
5 Which countries surround the Baltic Sea?
6 Name the countries these cities are the capitals of: Amsterdam, Athens, Berlin, Brussels, Copenhagen, Lisbon, London, Madrid, Moscow, Paris, Stockholm.
7 Which countries does the river Rhine flow through?
8 What does a political map show?

KEY

■ Capital city
• Other town or city
— Country boundary
〜 River

1 centimetre on the map measures
200 kilometres on the ground

0   200   400   600   800 km

0   1   2   3   4 cm

N
W   E
S

ARCTIC
OCEAN

ICELAND
Reykjavik

ATLANTIC
OCEAN

Arctic Circle

60°N

40°W   20°W   0°   20°E   40°E   80°N   60°E

80°N

60°E

Arctic Circle

NORWAY
Oslo

SWEDEN
Stockholm

FINLAND
Helsinki

L. Onega
L. Ladoga

St. Petersburg
Tallinn

RUSSIAN
FEDERATION

Moscow

60°N

ESTONIA

Baltic

LATVIA
Riga

Dvina

20°W

North

Sea

Sea

Edinburgh

UNITED
KINGDOM

IRELAND
Dublin

London

DENMARK
Copenhagen

LITHUANIA
Vilnius

R.F.

Minsk

BELORUSSIA

40°E

NETHERLANDS
Amsterdam
Rotterdam

Hamburg
Berlin

Vistula

Warsaw

Brussels
BELGIUM
Bonn

GERMANY

POLAND

Kiev

Seine

LUXEMBOURG

Rhine

Prague
CZECH
REPUBLIC   SLOVAKIA

UKRAINE

Dnieper

Paris

Loire

Munich

Vienna
Bratislava
Budapest

MOLDAVIA
Kishinev

Bay of
Biscay

FRANCE

Lyon

Berne
SWITZERLAND

Turin

AUSTRIA

HUNGARY

SLOVENIA
Ljubljana
Zagreb

Rhône

Po

Sava

CROATIA

ROMANIA

Belgrade

Bucharest

Black
Sea

Oporto

40°N

Lisbon

PORTUGAL

ANDORRA
Marseille

Barcelona   Corsica

Danube

BOSNIA-
HERZEGOVINA
Sarajevo

YUGO-
SLAVIA

BULGARIA
Sofia

40°N

SPAIN
Madrid
Valencia

Balearic Is.

Rome

ITALY

ALBANIA
Tiranë

Skopje
MACEDONIA

Istanbul

TURKEY

Naples

Sardinia

Gibraltar
(U.K.)

Mediterranean

Palermo

Sicily

GREECE

Athens

ASIA

Sea

Crete

AFRICA

MALTA

0°   20°E

41

The World - Countries

World map **A** is a **political map**. It shows the countries of the world and some major cities. You can see where the boundaries of the countries are and see which countries are next to each other. Map **B** shows the continents. You can work out which countries are in which continent.

There are nearly 200 countries in the world. They are all sorts of shapes and sizes. Some are very large, like the Russian Federation and Canada. Others are very small like Rwanda. Some are islands like Cuba. Others have no coastline like Mali. Find these countries on world map **A**.

KEY
■ Capital city
• Other major cities
— Country boundary

1 centimetre on the map measures
900 kilometres on the ground

Numbered countries
1 NETHERLANDS
2 BELGIUM
3 SWITZERLAND
4 AUSTRIA
5 CZECH REPUBLIC
6 HUNGARY

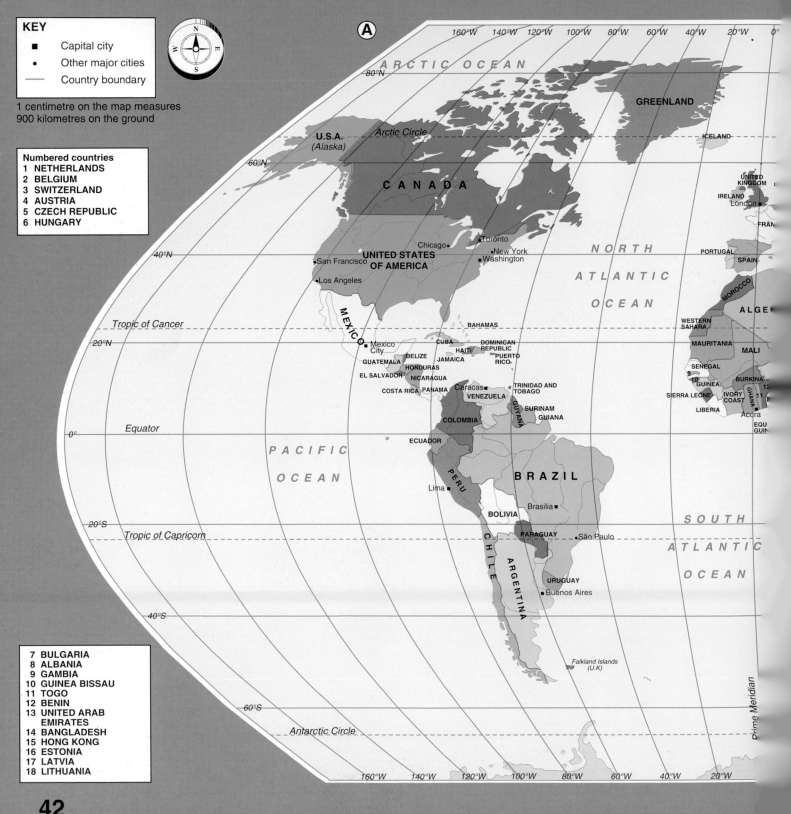

7 BULGARIA
8 ALBANIA
9 GAMBIA
10 GUINEA BISSAU
11 TOGO
12 BENIN
13 UNITED ARAB
   EMIRATES
14 BANGLADESH
15 HONG KONG
16 ESTONIA
17 LATVIA
18 LITHUANIA

1 Which countries have a border with Mali?
2 Name an island country apart from Cuba.
3 Name three countries which the Equator goes through.

4 Which continent has no countries in it?
5 Which continent contains most countries?
6 Is China nearer the USA if you travel east or if you travel west?

B

NORTH AMERICA · EUROPE · ASIA
AFRICA
SOUTH AMERICA
AUSTRALASIA
ANTARCTICA

19 ROMANIA
20 MOLDAVIA
21 GEORGIA
22 ARMENIA
23 AZERBAIJAN
24 TAJIKISTAN
25 YUGOSLAVIA
26 CROATIA
27 SLOVENIA
28 BOSNIA-HERZEGOVINA
29 LUXEMBOURG
30 ISRAEL
31 SLOVAKIA
32 MACEDONIA

The World - Physical features

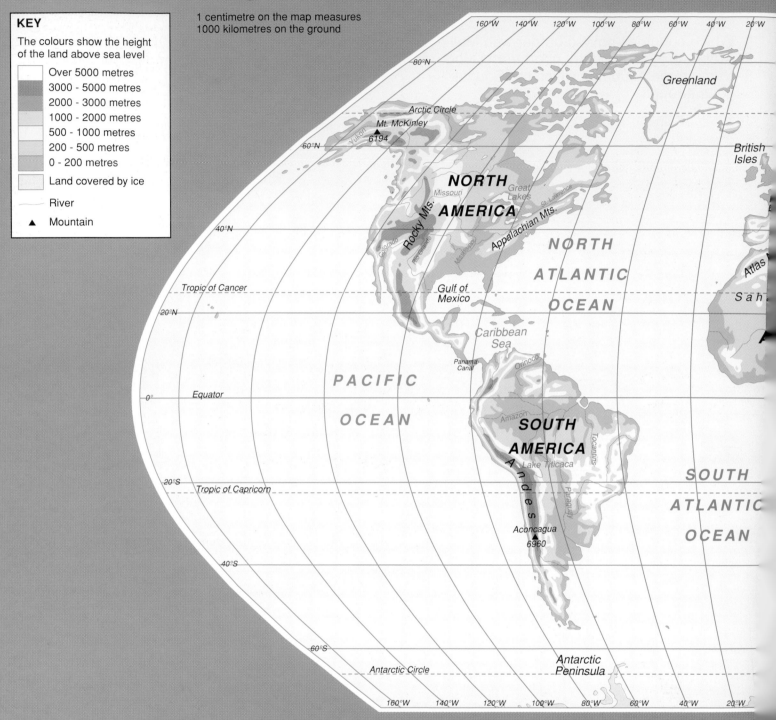

KEY

The colours show the height of the land above sea level

- Over 5000 metres
- 3000 - 5000 metres
- 2000 - 3000 metres
- 1000 - 2000 metres
- 500 - 1000 metres
- 200 - 500 metres
- 0 - 200 metres
- Land covered by ice
- River
- ▲ Mountain

1 centimetre on the map measures 1000 kilometres on the ground

This world map is a **physical map**. It shows how high the land is above sea level around the world. It names the main physical features of the world, such as the mountains, rivers, lakes, deserts, seas and islands.

On this world map you can see the equator. The equator divides the world into two halves. The half to the north of the equator is called the **northern hemisphere**. The half to the south of the equator is called the **southern hemisphere**.

The Prime Meridian also divides the world into two halves. To the west of the Prime Meridian is the **western hemisphere**. To the east of the Prime Meridian is the **eastern hemisphere**.

You can use the lines of latitude and longitude to give grid references. You can also name the hemisphere a place is in.

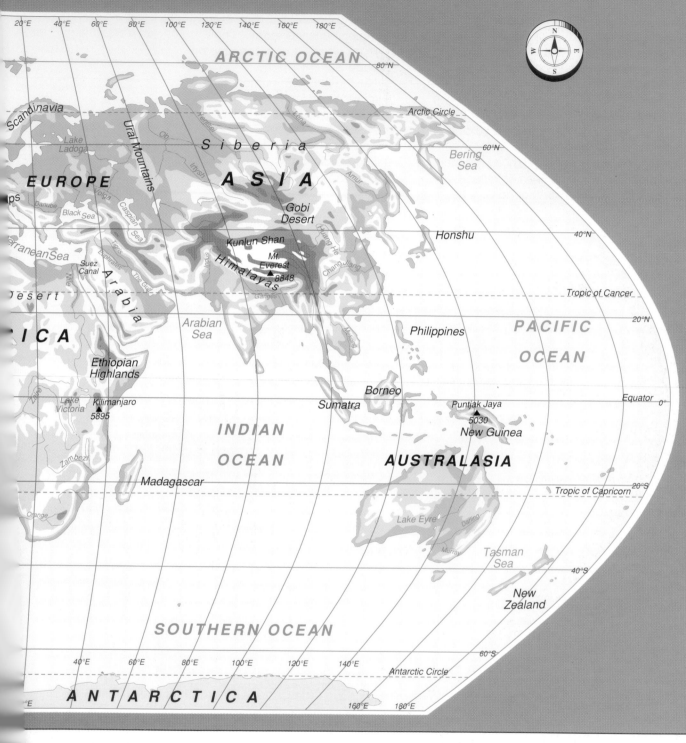

1 Is Europe in the northern or southern hemisphere?

2 Is Asia in the eastern or western hemisphere?

3 Which sea is at grid reference 15°N 75°W?

4 Which continents are on the western side of the Pacific Ocean?

5 Name the island southeast of Africa.

6 Which continent is in the northern and southern hemispheres **and** in the eastern and western hemispheres?

7 Which colour shows the lowest land that is above sea level?

8 Which mountain range runs along the western side of South America?

9 Give the grid reference for a mountain peak.

United Kingdom Index

A map **index** helps you to find out where places are on the map. On this page is the index for the United Kingdom maps on pages 28-31. On page 47 is the index for the maps of Europe and the World on pages 40-45. Most of the names on these maps are listed in the index.

The colour coding in the index will tell you whether the feature is water (blue), land (red) or man-made (black).

A grid has been drawn over each of the United Kingdom, Europe and World maps. It uses the lines of latitude and longitude. Each has been given a number and a letter. Part of one map is shown in **A**.

Here is part of the index:

> **Cambrian Mountains 31** 52N 3W
> **Cambridge** *town* **31** 52N 0
> **Cardiff** *town* **31** 51N 3W
> **Cardigan Bay 31** 52N 4W

To find Cardiff, first look it up in the alphabetical index. The index shows it is on the map on page 31.
Next to the page number is its latitude and longitude grid reference. This is 51N, 3W. Now turn to the correct page and use the grid reference to find Cardiff in the grid square on the map.

If you are not sure how to use latitude and longitude to find a grid reference, read pages 24-25, which explains how to do so.

Aberdeen *town* **28** 57N 2W
Aberystwyth *town* **31** 52N 4W
Anglesey *island* **31** 53N 4W
Arran *island* **29** 55N 5W

Ballymena *town* **29** 54N 6W
Bangor *town* **31** 53N 4W
Bann *river* **29** 55N 6W
Barnsley *town* **31** 53N 1W
Barrow-in-Furness *town* **30** 54N 3W
Basildon *town* **31** 51N 0
Basingstoke *town* **31** 51N 1W
Bath *town* **31** 51N 2W
Bedford *town* **31** 52N 0
Belfast *town* **29** 54N 5W
Ben Nevis *mountain* **28** 56N 5W
Berwick-upon-Tweed *town* **28** 55N 2W
Birkenhead *town* **31** 53N 3W
Birmingham *town* **31** 52N 1W
Blackburn *town* **30** 53N 2W
Blackpool *town* **30** 53N 3W
Bolton *town* **31** 53N 2W
Bournemouth *town* **31** 50N 1W
Bradford *town* **30** 53N 1W
Brighton *town* **31** 51N 0
Bristol *town* **31** 51N 2W

Cambrian Mountains 31 52N 3W
Cambridge *town* **31** 52N 0
Cardiff *town* **31** 51N 3W
Cardigan Bay 31 52N 4W
Carlisle *town* **30** 54N 2W
Channel Islands 31 49N 2W
Cheltenham *town* **31** 51N 2W
Chester *town* **31** 53N 2W
Cheviot Hills **29** 55N 2W
Chiltern Hills 31 51N 0
Clyde *river* **29** 55N 4W
Colwyn Bay *town* **31** 53N 3W
Cotswold Hills 31 51N 2W
Coventry *town* **31** 52N 1W
Crawley *town* **31** 51N 0
Crewe *town* **31** 53N 2W

Darlington *town* **30** 54N 1W
Dartmoor 31 50N 3W
Derby *town* **31** 52N 1W
Don *river* **28** 57N 2W
Doncaster *town* **31** 53N 1W
Douglas *town* **30** 54N 4W

Dumfries *town* **29** 55N 3W
Dundee *town* **28** 56N 2W
Dunfermline *town* **29** 56N 3W
Durham *town* **30** 54N 1W

Eastbourne *town* **31** 50N 0
Edinburgh *town* **29** 55N 3W
England *country* **31** 52N 1W
English Channel *sea* **31** 50N 1W
Erne *river* **29** 54N 7W
Exeter *town* **31** 50N 3W
Exmoor 31 51N 3W

Firth of Clyde 29 55N 4W
Folkestone *town* **31** 51N 1E
Forth *river* **29** 56N 3W
Fort William *town* **28** 56N 5W

Glasgow *town* **29** 55N 4W
Gloucester *town* **31** 51N 2W
Grampian Mountains 28 56N 4W
Greenock *town* **29** 55N 4W
Grimsby *town* **31** 49N 2W
Guernsey *island* **31** 49N 2W

Harlow *town* **31** 51N 0
Harris *island* **28** 57N 6W
Harrogate *town* **30** 53N 1W
Hastings *town* **31** 50N 0
Hebrides *islands* **28** 56N 6W
Hereford *town* **31** 52N 2W
Huddersfield *town* **31** 53N 1W
Hull *town* **30** 53N 0
Humber *river* **30** 53N 0

Inverness *town* **28** 57N 4W
Ipswich *town* **31** 52N 1E
Irish Sea 30 53N 4W
Isle of Man 30 54N 4W
Isle of Wight 31 50N 1W
Isles of Scilly 31 49N 6W

Jersey *island* **31** 49N 2W

Kirkwall *town* **28** 58N 2W

Lake District 30 54N 3W
Lancaster *town* **31** 54N 2W
Leeds *town* **30** 53N 1W
Leicester *town* **31** 52N 1W
Lerwick *town* **28** 60N 1W
Lewis *island* **28** 58N 6W
Lincoln *town* **31** 53N 0
Liverpool *town* **31** 53N 3W

Loch Lomond 29 56N 4W
Loch Ness 28 57N 4W
London *town* **31** 51N 0
Londonderry *town* **29** 55N 7W
Lough Neagh 29 54N 6W
Luton *town* **31** 51N 0

Macclesfield *town* **31** 53N 2W
Maidstone *town* **31** 51N 0
Manchester *town* **31** 53N 2W
Mansfield *town* **31** 53N 1W
Merthyr Tydfil *town* **31** 51N 3W
Middlesbrough *town* **30** 54N 1W
Milford Haven *town* **31** 51N 5W
Milton Keynes *town* **31** 52N 0
Motherwell *town* **29** 55N 3W
Mourne *river* **29** 54N 7W
Mourne Mountains 29 54N 6W
Mull *island* **28** 56N 6W

Newcastle *town* **30** 54N 1W
Newport *town* **31** 51N 2W
Newry *town* **29** 54N 6W
Northampton *town* **31** 52N 0
Northern Ireland *country* **29** 54N 7W
North Sea 28 56N 3E
North Uist *island* **28** 57N 7W
Northwest Highlands *mountains* **28** 57N 5W
Norwich *town* **31** 52N 1E
Nottingham *town* **31** 52N 1W

Oban *town* **28** 56N 5W
Orkney Islands 28 59N 3W
Ouse *river* **31** 52N 0
Oxford *town* **31** 51N 1W

Pennines *hills* **30** 54N 2W
Pentland Firth 28 58N 3W
Penzance *town* **31** 50N 5W
Perth *town* **28** 56N 3W
Peterborough *town* **31** 52N 0
Plymouth *town* **31** 50N 4W
Portadown *town* **29** 54N 6W
Portsmouth *town* **31** 50N 1W
Preston *town* **30** 53N 2W

Reading *town* **31** 51N 0
Rugby *town* **31** 52N 1W

Scafell Pike *mountain* **30** 54N 3W
Scarborough *town* **30** 54N 0

Scotland *country* **28** 57N 4W
Severn *river* **31** 51N 2W
Sheffield *town* **31** 53N 1W
Shetland Islands 28 60N 1W
Shrewsbury *town* **31** 52N 2W
Skye *island* **28** 57N 6W
Slieve Donard *mountain* **29** 54N 5W
Snowdon *mountain* **31** 53N 4W
Southampton *town* **31** 50N 1W
Southend *town* **31** 51N 0
Southern Uplands *hills* **29** 55N 3W
South Uist *island* **28** 57N 7W
Spey *river* **28** 57N 3W
Stirling *town* **29** 56N 3W
Stockport *town* **31** 53N 2W
Stoke *town* **31** 53N 2W
Stornoway *town* **28** 58N 6W
Stranraer *town* **29** 54N 5W
Sunderland *town* **30** 54N 1W
Swansea *town* **31** 51N 3W
Swindon *town* **31** 51N 3W

Tees *river* **30** 54N 2W
Telford *town* **31** 52N 2W
Thames *river* **31** 51N 0
The Fens 31 52N 0
The Wash 31 52N 0
Thurso *town* **28** 58N 3W
Torbay *town* **31** 50N 3W
Trent *river* **31** 52N 1W
Tweed *river* **29** 55N 2W
Tyne *river* **30** 55N 1W

Wales *country* **31** 52N 3W
Walsall *town* **31** 52N 1W
Warrington *town* **31** 53N 2W
Watford *town* **31** 51N 0
Weston-super-Mare *town* **31** 51N 2W
Weymouth *town* **31** 50N 2W
Wick *town* **28** 58N 3W
Wigan *town* **31** 53N 2W
Wolverhampton *town* **31** 52N 2W
Worcester *town* **31** 52N 2W
Workington *town* **30** 54N 3W
Wrexham *town* **31** 53N 3W
Wye *river* **31** 52N 2W

York *town* **30** 53N 1W
Yorkshire Moors *hills* **31** 54N 0

World Index

Teacher's Notes

MAPSKILLS

Ideas / Skills	Resources	Extension Activities	Nat Cur Geo POS Links
2-3 **Use pictures and photos to identify and to find out about places. Identify features on vertical aerial photos and match them to a map. Interpret symbols. Follow routes on a map.**	• photos of features in school local area • oblique/vertical photos of school area • large scale OS map of local area • photos/large scale maps of other areas, eg where go on school journeys/fieldtrips	• use OS map and walk round local area locating features, noting how shown on map, updating map • follow route around local area using map • make a model of the area around the school • devise shortest routes from school to local places • compare aerial photos and maps	KS2 / 3d KS2 / 3e KS2 / 5a KS2 / 3d
4 **Use four-figure grid references to locate features on a map.** • use of smaller scale map	• use of local area map with grid overlay to practise grid references • grid sheets with numbers marked	• on grid sheets, children mark list of grid references, then join them up to produce a shape • play battleships	KS2 / 3d
5 **Use the eight points of the compass.** • use 4 and 8 compass points • reinforce idea of symbols and key • use of smaller scale map: OS 1:10 000	• OS maps of local area, including 1:10 000 • directional compasses: large for demonstration, small for personal use	• give and follow compass directions walking round the playground,school • orient local map to area using compass • give and follow compass directions on map	KS2 / 3d
6-7 **Determine the straight line distance between two points on a map. Understand the notion of scale in maps.** • use of a scale bar	• plans of objects in room, room plans, school plans all drawn to scale • OS large scale map of area, 1:1250 or 1:2500	• measure distances on plans/maps using scale bar • draw scale plans of objects, rooms, school, grounds: discuss best scale	KS2 / 3d

USING MAPS

Ideas / Skills	Resources	Extension Activities	Nat Cur Geo POS Links
8-9 **Investigate the use of land and buildings in the local area.** • use of a base map in a local area survey • classification of services by function	• base map of local shopping streets • photos of local shops/other features • copies of any survey maps of local shops undertaken in the past	• make a survey of the local shopping streets/area annotating the base map • classify shops types and make classification map, graphs and charts to show variety	KS2 / 2b KS2 / 2c KS2 / 3d
10-11 **Change in a local community over a short period of time.** • use of map to show that changes have happened and can be planned • ideas of change and continuity	• old and current large scale OS maps of local area • old and current photos of features/streets in local area • other old maps of local area	• use old local area map to find the way around • use old map to model how area once looked • on OHP lay transparency of current map over old map to see where change has occured • make plans of how the area could develop	KS2 / 3d KS2 / 5d
12-13 **Plan and follow routes using maps. Why different means of transport may be used.** • use of street, bus and rail maps in journey planning	• local street maps or street atlas, and OS 1:10 000 map • street, bus and rail maps for local area and other places visited on school journeys/fieldwork	• collect maps intended for route planning • discuss why it may be necessary to use different forms of transport during a journey • use maps in planning imaginary journeys, eg as travel agents/tour operators	KS2 / 3d

LANDSHAPE

Ideas / Skills	Resources	Extension Activities	Nat Cur Geo POS Links
14-15 **Interpret relief maps.** • cartographers have used different ways to show hills and slopes on maps: hillocks, hachures, hillshading	• photos and pictures of hilly landscapes • postcards and picture maps using hillocks as symbols for hilly landscapes • local street map	• discuss changes in way hills shown on maps • use local street map, work out way of showing slope of ground: where, how much, direction • make, then map, model of undulating landscape	KS2 / 3d KS3 / 3d
16 **Interpret relief maps.** • idea of relative height: higher/lower than • idea of slope and direction • idea of layer-coloured maps	• local area OS 1:10 000 map • photos of slope/relief features • OS 1:10 000 maps of areas used for field trips	• identify features that indicate slopes in photos and on OS maps • using base map survey local streets to record which slope up/down hill from school	KS2 / 3d KS2 / 3e KS2 / 5a KS3 / 3d
17 **Interpret relief maps.** • idea of absolute height of land • spot height as symbol to show height • contours show shape, height, slope	• OS 1:10 000 maps of local and other areas, showing contours • photos/drawings of slopes/hills, and contour maps to match, showing shape	• from map describe walk on a route, saying whether going up/down hill, slope gentle/steep then walk area where contour lines show slope • make a contour-layer model of the local area	

DECREASING SCALES

Ideas / Skills	Resources	Extension Activities	Nat Cur Geo POS Links
18-19 **Use six-figure grid references to locate features on a map. Use conventional 1:25 000 and 1:50 000 OS map symbols with the aid of a key. Follow a route on an OS map and describe what would be seen.** • origin of settlement names in an area	• OS 1:25 000 and 1:50 000 scale maps of local area and other localities • centimetre ruler • reference book on place names and meanings	• use the key to work out what the symbols show, and identify a variety of features in a grid square • use OS maps to practice grid references • look for patterns of contour lines to see what features are shown, eg hills, valleys • make a list of local names from OS map and find out their origin/meaning	KS2 / 3d KS2 / 5a KS3 / 3d